DATE DUE

NOV 4 1992	
DEC 1 3 1996	
MAR 1 9 2001	
APR 0 2 2001	
APR 0 4 2006	
MAY 1 4 2010	
DEC 0 7 2010	

Modern Critical Views

EDGAR ALLAN POE

Modern Critical Views

EDGAR ALLAN POE

Edited with an introduction by

Harold Bloom

Sterling Professor of the Humanities
Yale University

1985
CHELSEA HOUSE PUBLISHERS
New York

PROJECT EDITORS: Emily Bestler, James Uebbing
EDITORIAL COORDINATOR: Karyn Browne
EDITORIAL STAFF: Sally Stepanek, Linda Grossman
RESEARCH: Marena Fisher
DESIGN: Susan Lusk

Cover illustration by Kye Carbone
Composition provided by Collage Publications, Inc., New York

Library of Congress Cataloging in Publication Data
Edgar Allan Poe, modern critical views.
    Bibliography: p.
    Contents: Introduction: Americanizing the Abyss/
Harold Bloom—On Poe's *Eureka*/Paul Valéry—Edgar
Allan Poe/D.H. Lawrence—[etc.]
    1. Poe, Edgar Allan, 1809–1849—Criticism and
interpretation—Addresses, essays, lectures. I. Bloom,
Harold.
PS2638.E32   1984   818'.309   84-22929
ISBN 0–87754–602–9

Contents

Editor's Note

The essays in this collection are arranged in the order of their composition. They chronicle the most advanced criticism that Poe has received. I have placed emphasis upon *Eureka*, the tales, and *Pym*, but the final essay by Shoshana Felman is also a defense of Poe's stance as a poet, returning us full circle to the speculations of Valéry.

Introduction

I

Valéry, in a letter to Gide, asserted that "Poe is the only impeccable writer. He was never mistaken." If this judgment startles an American reader, it is less remarkable than Baudelaire's habit of making his morning prayers to God and to Edgar Poe. If we add the devotion of Mallarmé to what he called his master Poe's "severe ideas," then we have some sense of the scandal of what might be called "French Poe," perhaps as much a Gallic mystification as "French Freud." French Poe is less bizarre than French Freud, but more puzzling, because its literary authority ought to be overwhelming, and yet vanishes utterly when confronted by what Poe actually wrote. Here is the second stanza of the impeccable writer's celebrated lyric, "For Annie":

> Sadly, I know
> I am shorn of my strength,
> And no muscle I move
> As I lie at full length—
> But no matter!—I feel
> I am better at length.

Though of a badness not to be believed, this is by no means unrepresentative of Poe's verse. Aldous Huxley charitably supposed that Baudelaire, Mallarmé and Valéry simply had no ear for English, and so just could not hear Poe's palpable vulgarity. Nothing even in Poe's verse is so wickedly funny as Huxley's parody in which a grand Miltonic touchstone is transmuted into the mode of Poe's "Ulalume." First Milton, in *Paradise Lost*, IV, 268–273:

> Not that fair field
> Of Enna, where Proserpine gathering flowers
> Her self a fairer flower by gloomy Dis
> Was gathered, which cost Ceres all that pain
> To seek her through the world;

From *The New York Review of Books*, Vol. 31, No. 15. Copyright © 1984 by *The New York Review of Books*.

Next, Huxley's Poe:

> It was noon in the fair field of Enna,
>> When Proserpina gathering flowers—
>> Herself the most fragrant of flowers,
> Was gathered away to Gehenna
>> By the Prince of Plutonian powers;
> Was borne down the windings of Brenner
>> To the gloom of his amorous bowers—
> Down the tortuous highway of Brenner
>> To the God's agapemonous bowers.

What then did Baudelaire hear, what music of thought, when he read the actual Poe of "Ulalume"?

> Here once, through an alley Titanic,
>> Of cypress, I roamed with my Soul—
>> Of cypress, with Psyche, my Soul.
> These were days when my heart was volcanic
>> As the scoriac rivers that roll—
>> As the lavas that restlessly roll
> Their sulphurous currents down Yaanek,
>> In the ultimate climes of the Pole—
> That groan as they roll down Mount Yaanek,
>> In the realms of the Boreal Pole.

If this were Edward Lear, poet of "The Dong with the Luminous Nose" or "The Jumblies," one might not question Baudelaire and the other apostles of French Poe. But the hard-driven Poe did not set out to write nonsense verse. His desire was to be the American Coleridge or Byron or Shelley, and his poetry, at its rare best, echoes those High Romantic forerunners with some grace and a certain plangent urgency. Yet even "The City in the Sea" is a touch too close to Byron's "Darkness," while "Israfel" weakly revises Shelley's "To a Skylark." Nineteenth century American poetry is considerably better than it is generally acknowledged to be. There are no other figures comparable to Whitman and Dickinson, but at least the following are clearly preferable to Poe, taking them chronologically: Bryant, Emerson, Longfellow, Whittier, Jones Very, Thoreau, Melville, Timrod and Tuckerman. Poe scrambles for twelfth place with Sidney Lanier; if this judgment seems harsh, or too arithmetical, it is prompted by the continued French overvaluation of Poe as lyricist. No reader who cares deeply for the best poetry written in English can care greatly for Poe's verse. Huxley's accusation of vulgarity and bad taste is just: "To the most sensitive and high-souled man in the world we should find it hard to forgive, shall we say, the wearing of a diamond ring on every finger. Poe does the equivalent of this in his poetry; we notice the solecism and shudder."

II

Whatever his early ambitions, Poe wrote relatively little verse; there are scarcely a hundred pages of it in the remarkable new edition of his complete writings, in two substantial volumes, published by The Library of America. The bulk of his work is in tale-telling and criticism, with the exception of the problematic *Eureka: A Prose Poem,* a hundred page cosmology that I take to be Poe's answer to Emerson's Transcendental manifesto, *Nature.* Certainly *Eureka* is more of a literary achievement than Poe's verse, while the popularity and influence of the shorter tales has been and remains immense. Whether either *Eureka* or the famous stories can survive authentic criticism is not clear, but nothing could remove the stories from the canon anyway. They are a permanent element in Western literary culture, even though they are best read when we are very young. Poe's criticism has mixed repute, but in fact has never been made fully available until The Library of America edition.

Poe's survival raises perpetually the issue as to whether literary merit and canonical status necessarily go together. I can think of no other American writer, down to this moment, at once so inevitable and so dubious. Mark Twain catalogued Fenimore Cooper's literary offenses, but all that he exuberantly listed are minor compared to Poe's. Allen Tate, proclaiming Poe "our cousin" in 1949, at the centenary of Poe's death, remarked: "He has several styles, and it is not possible to damn them all at once." Uncritical admirers of Poe should be asked to read his stories aloud (but only to themselves!). The association between the acting style of Vincent Price and the styles of Poe is alas not gratuitous, and indeed is an instance of deep crying out unto deep. Lest I be considered unfair by those devoted to Poe, I hasten to quote him at his strongest as a storyteller. Here is the opening paragraph of "William Wilson," a tale admired by Dostoevsky and still central to the great Western topos of the double:

> Let me call myself, for the present, William Wilson. The fair page now lying before me need not be sullied with my real appellation. This has been already too much an object for the scorn—for the horror—for the detestation of my race. To the uttermost regions of the globe have not the indignant winds bruited its unparalleled infamy? Oh, outcast of all outcasts most abandoned!—to the earth art thou not forever dead? to its honors, to its flowers, to its golden aspirations?—and a cloud, dense, dismal, and limitless, does it not hang eternally between thy hopes and heaven?

This rhetoric, including the rhetorical questions, is British Gothic rather than German Gothic, Ossian or Monk Lewis rather than Tieck or E.T.A. Hoffmann. Its palpable squalors require no commentary. The critical question surely must be: how does "William Wilson" survive its bad writing? Poe's awful diction, whether here or in "The Fall of the House of Usher" or "The Purloined Letter" seems to demand the decent masking of a competent French translation. The tale somehow is stronger than its telling, which is to say that Poe's actual text does not matter. What survives, despite Poe's writing, are the psychological dynamics and mythic reverberations of his stories about William Wilson and Roderick Usher. Poe can only gain by a good translation, and scarcely loses if each reader fully retells the stories to another. C.S. Lewis, defending the fantasies of George Macdonald (*George Macdonald: An Anthology* by C.S. Lewis, Doubleday Dolphin Books, 1962), formulated a curious principle that seems to me more applicable to Poe than to Macdonald:

> The texture of his writing as a whole is undistinguished, at times fumbling . . . But this does not quite dispose of him even for the literary critic. What he does best is fantasy—fantasy that hovers between the allegorical and the mythopoeic. And this, in my opinion, he does better than any man. The critical problem with which we are confronted is whether this art—the art of mythmaking—is a species of the literary art. The objection to so classifying it is that the Myth does not essentially exist in words at all. We all agree that the story of Balder is a great myth, a thing of inexhaustible value. But of whose version—whose *words*—are we thinking when we say this?

Lewis replies that he is not thinking of anyone's words, but of a particular pattern of events. Of course that means Lewis is thinking of his own words. He goes so far as to remember:

> . . . when I first heard the story of Kafka's *Castle* related in conversation and afterwards read the book for myself. The reading added nothing. I had already received the myth, which was all that mattered.

Clearly mistaken about Kafka, Lewis was certainly correct about Macdonald's *Lilith*, and I think the insight is valid for Poe's stories. Myths matter because we prefer them in our own words, and so Poe's diction scarcely distracts us from our retelling, to ourselves, his bizarre myths. There is a dreadful universalism pervading Poe's weird tales. The Freudian reductions of Marie Bonaparte pioneered at converting Poe's universalism into the psychoanalytical universalism, but Poe is himself so reductive that the Freudian translations are in his case merely redundant. Poe authentically frightens children, and the fright can be a kind of trauma. I remember reading Poe's tales and Bram Stoker's *Dracula*, each for the first time, when I was about ten. *Dracula* I shrugged off (at least until I confronted Bela Lugosi murmuring: "I never drink—wine!") but Poe induced nasty and repetitious nightmares that linger even now. Myth may be only what the Polish aphorist Stanislaw Lec once called it, "gossip grown old," but then Poe would have to be called a very vivid gossip, though not often a very eloquent one.

III

Critics, even good ones, admire Poe's stories for some of the oddest of reasons. Poe, a true Southerner, abominated Emerson, plainly perceiving that Emerson (like Whitman, like Lincoln) was not a Christian, not a royalist, not a classicist. Self-reliance, the Emersonian answer to Original Sin, does not exist in the Poe cosmos, where you necessarily start out damned, doomed and dismal. But I think Poe detested Emerson for some of the same reasons Hawthorne and Melville more subtly resented him, reasons that persist in the most distinguished living American writer, Robert Penn Warren, and in many current academic literary critics in our country. If you dislike Emerson, you probably will like Poe. Emerson fathered pragmatism; Poe fathered precisely nothing, which is the way he would have wanted it. Yvor Winters accused Poe of obscurantism, but that truthful indictment no more damages Poe than does tastelessness and tone-deafness. Emerson, for better and for worse, was and is the mind of America, but Poe was and is our hysteria, our uncanny unanimity in our repressions. I certainly do not intend to mean by this that Poe was deeper than Emerson in any way whatsoever. Emerson cheerfully and consciously threw out the past. Critics tend to share Poe's easy historicism; perhaps without knowing it, they are gratified that every Poe story is, in too clear a sense, over even as it begins. We don't have to wait for Madeline Usher and the house to fall in upon poor Roderick; they have fallen in upon him already, before the narrator comes upon the place. Emerson exalted freedom, which he and Thoreau usefully called "wildness." No one in Poe is or can be free or wild, and some academic admirers of Poe truly like everything and everyone to be in bondage to a universal past. To begin is to be free, god-like and Emersonian-Adamic, or Jeffersonian. But for a writer to be free is bewildering and even maddening. What American writers and their exegetes half-unknowingly love in Poe is his more-than-Freudian oppressive and curiously original sense and sensation of overdetermination. Walter Pater once remarked that museums depressed him because they made him doubt that anyone ever had once been young. No one in a Poe story ever was young. As D. H. Lawrence angrily observed, everyone in Poe is a vampire—Poe himself in particular.

IV

Among Poe's tales, the near-exception to what I have been saying is the longest and most ambitious, *The Narrative of Arthur Gordon Pym*, just as the best of Poe's poems is the long prose-poem, *Eureka*. Alas, even these works are somewhat over-valued, if only because Poe's critics understandably become excessively eager to see him vindicated. *Pym* is readable, but *Eureka* is extravagantly repetitious. Auden was quite taken with *Eureka*, but could remember very little of it in conversation, and one can doubt that he read it through, at least in English. Poe's most advanced critic is John T. Irwin, in his book *American Hieroglyphics* (New Haven, 1980; paperback edition, Baltimore, 1983). Irwin rightly centers upon *Pym*, while defending *Eureka* as an "aesthetic cosmology" addressed to what in each of us Freud called the "bodily ego." Irwin is too shrewd to assert that Poe's performance in *Eureka* fulfills Poe's extraordinary intentions:

> What the poem *Eureka*, at once pre-Socratic and post-Newtonian, asserts is the truth of the feeling, the bodily intuition, that the diverse objects which the mind discovers in contemplating external nature form a unity, that they are all parts of one body which, if not infinite, is so gigantic as to be beyond both the spatial and temporal limits of human perception. In *Eureka*, then, Poe presents us with the paradox of a "unified" macrocosmic body that is without a totalizing image—an alogical, intuitive belief whose "truth" rests upon Poe's sense that cosmologies and myths of origin are forms of internal geography that, under the guise of mapping the physical universe, map the universe of desire.

Irwin might be writing of Blake, or of other visionaries who have sought to map total forms of desire. What Irwin catches, by implication, is Poe's troubling anticipation of what is most difficult in Freud, the "frontier concepts" between mind and body, such as the bodily ego, the non-repressive defense of introjection, and above all, the drives or instincts. Poe, not just in *Eureka* and in *Pym*, but throughout his tales and even in some of his verse, is peculiarly close to the Freudian speculation upon the bodily ego. Freud, in *The Ego and the Id* (1923), resorted to the uncanny language of E.T.A. Hoffman (and of Poe) in describing this difficult notion:

> The ego is first and foremost a bodily ego; it is not merely a surface entity, but is itself the projection of a surface. If we wish to find an anatomical analogy for it we can best identify it with the 'cortical homunculus' of the anatomists, which stands on its head in the cortex, sticks up its heels, faces backwards and, as we know, has its speech-area on the left-hand side.

A footnote in the English translation of 1927, authorized by Freud but never added to the German editions, elucidates the first sentence of this description in a way analogous to the crucial metaphor in Poe that concludes *The Narrative of Arthur Gordon Pym*:

> I.e. the ego is ultimately derived from bodily sensations, chiefly from those springing from the surface of the body, besides, as we have seen above, representing the superficies of the mental apparatus.

A considerable part of Poe's mythological power emanates from his own difficult sense that the ego is always a bodily ego. The characters of Poe's tales live out nearly every conceivable fantasy of introjection and identification, seeking to assuage their melancholia by psychically devouring the lost objects of their affections. D.H. Lawrence, in his *Studies in Classic American Literature* (1923), moralized powerfully against Poe, condemning him for "the will-to-love and the will-to-consciousness, asserted against death itself. The pride of human conceit in KNOWLEDGE." It is illuminating that Lawrence attacked Poe in much the same spirit as he attacked Freud, who is interpreted in *Psychoanalysis and the Unconscious* as somehow urging us to violate the taboo against incest. The interpretation is as extravagant as Lawrence's thesis that Poe urged vampirism upon us, but there remains something suggestive in Lawrence's violence against both Freud and Poe. Each placed the elitist individual in jeopardy, Lawrence implied, by hinting at the primacy of fantasy not just in the sexual life proper, but in the bodily ego's constitution of itself through acts of incorporation and identification.

The cosmology of *Eureka* and the narrative of *Pym* alike circle around fantasies of incorporation. *Eureka*'s subtitle is "An Essay on the Material and Spiritual Universe" and what Poe calls its "general proposition" is heightened by italics: *"In the Original Unity of the First Thing lies the Secondary Cause of all Things, with the Germ of their Inevitable Annihilation."* Freud, in his cosmology, *Beyond the Pleasure Principle*, posited that the inorganic had preceded the organic, and also that it was the tendency of all things to return to their original state. Consequently, the aim of all life was death. The death drive, which became crucial for Freud's later dualisms, is nevertheless pure mythology, since Freud's only evidence for it was the repetition compulsion, and it is an extravagant leap from repetition to death. This reliance upon one's own mythology may have prompted Freud's audacity when, in the *New Introductory Lectures*, he admitted that the theory of drives was, so to speak, his own mythology, drives being not only magnificent conceptions but particularly sublime in their indefiniteness. I wish I could assert that *Eureka* has some of the speculative force of *Beyond the Pleasure Principle* or even of Freud's disciple Ferenczi's startling *Thalassa: A Theory of Genitality*, but *Eureka* does badly enough when compared to Emerson's *Nature*, which itself has only a few passages worthy of what Emerson wrote afterwards. And yet Valéry in one sense was justified in his praise for *Eureka*. For certain intellectuals, *Eureka* performs a mythological function akin to what Poe's tales continue to do for hosts of readers. *Eureka* is unevenly written, badly repetitious, and sometimes opaque in its abstractness, but like the tales it seems not to have been composed by a particular individual. The universalism of a common nightmare informs it. If the tales lose little, or even gain, when we retell them to others in our own words, *Eureka* gains by Valéry's observations, or by the summaries of recent critics like John Irwin or Daniel Hoffman. Translation even into his own language always benefits Poe.

I haven't the space, or the desire, to summarize *Eureka*, and no summary is likely to do anything besides deadening both my readers and myself. Certainly Poe was never more passionately sincere than in composing *Eureka*, of which he affirmed: *"What I here propound is true."* But these are the closing sentences of *Eureka*:

> Think that the sense of individual identity will be gradually merged in the general consciousness—that Man, for example, ceasing imperceptibly to feel himself Man, will at length attain that awfully triumphant epoch when he shall recognize his existence as that of Jehovah. In the meantime bear in mind that all is Life—Life—Life within Life—the less within the greater, and all within the *Spirit Divine*.

To this, Poe appends a "Note":

> The pain of the consideration that we shall lose our individual identity, ceases at once when we further reflect that the process, as above described, is, neither more nor less than that of the absorption, by each individual intelligence, of all other intelligences (that is, of the Universe) into its own. That God may be all in all, *each* must become God.

Allen Tate, not unsympathetic to his cousin, Mr. Poe, remarked of Poe's extinction in *Eureka* that "there is a lurid sublimity in the spectacle of his taking God along with him into a grave which is not smaller than the universe." If we read closely, Poe's trope is "absorption," and we are where we always are in Poe, amid ultimate fantasies of introjection in which the bodily ego and the cosmos become indistinguishable. That makes Poe the most cannibalistic of authors, and seems less a function of his "angelic" theological imagination than of his mechanisms of defense. Again, I suspect this judgment hardly weakens Poe, since his strength is no more cognitive than it is stylistic. Poe's mythology, like the mythology of psychoanalysis that we cannot yet bear to acknowledge as primarily a mythology, is peculiarly appropriate to any modernism, whether you want to call it early, high or post-modernism. The definitive judgment belongs here to T.W. Adorno, certainly the most authentic theoretician of all modernisms, in his last book, *Aesthetic Theory* (translated by C. Lenhardt, Routledge & Kegan Paul, London and Boston, 1948). Writing on "reconciliation and mimetic adaptation to death, " Adorno blends the insights of Jewish negative theology and psychoanalysis:

> Whether negativity is the barrier or the truth of art is not for art to decide. Art works are negative *per se* because they are subject to the law of objectification; that is, they kill what they objectify, tearing it away from its context of immediacy and real life. They survive because they bring death.

This is particularly true of modern art, where we notice a general mimetic abandonment to reification, which is the principle of death. Illusion in art is the attempt to escape from this principle. Baudelaire marks a watershed, in that art after him seeks to discard illusion without resigning itself to being a thing among things. The harbingers of modernism, Poe and Baudelaire, were the first technocrats of art.

Baudelaire was more than a technocrat of art, as Adorno knew, but Poe would be only that except for his myth-making gift. C.S. Lewis may have been right when he insisted that such a gift could exist even apart from other literary endowments. Blake and Freud are inescapable myth-makers who were also cognitively and stylistically powerful. Poe is a great fantasist whose thoughts were commonplace and whose metaphors were dead. Fantasy, mythologically considered, combines the stances of Narcissus and Prometheus, which are ideologically antithetical to one another, but figuratively quite compatible. Poe is at once the Narcissus and the Prometheus of his nation. If that is right, then he is inescapable, even though his tales contrast weakly with Hawthorne's, his poems scarcely bear reading, and his speculative discourses fade away in juxtaposition to Emerson's, his despised Northern rival.

V

To define Poe's mythopoeic inevitability more closely, I turn to his story, "Ligeia," and to the end of *Pym*. Ligeia, a tall, dark, slender transcendentalist, dies murmuring a protest against the feeble human will, which cannot keep us forever alive. Her distraught and nameless widower, the narrator, endeavors to comfort himself, first with opium, and then with a second bride, "the fair-haired and blue-eyed Lady Rowena Trevanian, of Tremaine." Unfortunately, he has little use for this replacement, and so she sickens rapidly and dies. Recurrently, the corpse revivifies, only to die yet again and again. At last, the cerements are stripped away, and the narrator confronts the undead Ligeia, attired in the death-draperies of her now evaporated successor.

As a parable of the vampiric will, this works well enough. The learned Ligeia presumably has completed her training in the will during her absence, or perhaps merely owes death a substitute, the insufficiently transcendental Rowena. What is mythopoeically more impressive is the ambiguous question of the narrator's will. Poe's own life, like Walt Whitman's, is an American mythology, and what all of us generally remember about it is that Poe married his first cousin, Virginia Clemm, before she turned fourteen. She died a little more than ten years later, having been a semi-invalid for most of that time.

Poe himself died less than three years after her, when he was just forty. "Ligeia," regarded by Poe as his best tale, was written a bit more than a year into the marriage. The later Freud implicitly speculates that there are no accidents; we die because we will to die, our character being also our fate. In Poe's myth also, ethos is the daemon, and the daemon is our destiny. The year after Virginia died, Poe proposed marriage to the widowed poet Sarah Helen Whitman. Biographers tell us that the lady's doubts were caused by rumors of Poe's bad character, but perhaps Mrs. Whitman had read "Ligeia"! In any event, this marriage did not take place, nor did Poe survive to marry another widow, his childhood sweetheart Elmira Royster Skelton. Perhaps she too might have read "Ligeia" and forborne.

The narrator of "Ligeia" has a singularly bad memory, or else a very curious relationship to his own will, since he begins by telling us that he married Ligeia without ever having troubled to learn her family name. Her name itself is legend, or romance, and that was enough. As the story's second paragraph hints, the lady was an opium dream with the footfall of a shadow. The implication may be that there never was such a lady, or even that if you wish to incarnate your reveries, then you must immolate your consubstantial Rowena. What is a touch alarming, to the narrator, is the intensity of Ligeia's passion for him, which was manifested however only by glances and voice so long as the ideal lady lived. Perhaps this baffled intensity is what kills Ligeia, through a kind of narcissistic dialectic, since she is dominated not by the will of her lust but by the lust of her will. She wills her infinite passion towards the necessarily inadequate narrator and when (by implication) he fails her, she turns the passion of her will against dying and at last against death. Her dreadful poem, "The Conqueror Worm," prophesies her cyclic return from death: "Through a circle that ever returneth in / To the self-same spot." But when she does return, the spot is hardly the same. Poor Rowena only becomes even slightly interesting to her narrator-husband when she sickens unto death, and her body is wholly usurped by the revived Ligeia. And yet the wretched narrator is a touch different, if only because his narcissism is finally out of balance with his first wife's grisly Prometheanism. There are no final declarations of Ligeia's passion as the story concludes. The triumph of her will is complete, but we know that the narrator's will has not blent itself into Ligeia's. His renewed obsession with her eyes testifies to a continued sense of her daemonic power over him, but his final words hint at what the story's opening confirms: she will not be back for long—and remains "my lost love."

The conclusion of *Pym* has been brilliantly analyzed by John Irwin, and so I want to glance only briefly at what is certainly Poe's most effective closure:

> And now we rushed into the embraces of the cataract, where a chasm threw
> itself open to receive us. But there arose in our pathway a shrouded human

figure, very far larger in its proportions than any dweller among men. And the hue of the skin of the figure was of the perfect whiteness of the snow.

Irwin demonstrates Poe's reliance here upon the Romantic topos of the Alpine White Shadow, the magnified projection of the observer himself. The chasm Pym enters is the familiar Romantic Abyss, not a part of the natural world but belonging to eternity, before the creation. Reflected in that abyss, Pym beholds his own shrouded form, perfect in the whiteness of the natural context. Presumably, this is the original bodily ego, the Gnostic self before the fall into creation. As at the close of *Eureka*, Poe brings Alpha and Omega together in an apocalyptic circle. I suggest we read Pym's, which is to say Poe's, white shadow as the American triumph of the will, as illusory as Ligeia's usurpation of Rowena's corpse.

Poe teaches us, through Pym and Ligeia, that as Americans we are both subject and object of our own quests. Emerson, in Americanizing the European sense of the abyss, kept the self and the abyss separate as facts: "There may be two or three or four steps, according to the genius of each, but for every seeing soul there are two absorbing facts—I and the Abyss." Poe, seeking to avoid Emersonianism, ends with only one fact, and it is more a wish than a fact: "I will to be the Abyss." This metaphysical despair has appealed to the Southern American literary tradition and to its Northern followers. The appeal cannot be refuted, because it is myth, and Poe backed the myth with his life as well as his work. If the Northern or Emersonian myth of our literary culture culminates in the beautiful image of Walt Whitman as wound-dresser, moving as a mothering father through the Civil War Washington, D.C. hospitals, then the Southern or counter-myth achieves its perfect stasis at its start, with Poe's snow-white shadow shrouding the chasm down which the boat of the soul is about to plunge. Poe's genius was for negativity and opposition, and the affirmative force of Emersonian America gave him the impetus his daemonic will required.

VI

It would be a relief to say that Poe's achievement as a critic is not mythological, but the splendid, new and almost complete edition of his essays, reviews and marginalia testifies otherwise. It shows Poe indeed to have been Adorno's "technocrat of art." Auden defended Poe's criticism by contrasting the subjects Baudelaire was granted—Delacroix, Constantin Guys, Wagner—with the books Poe was given to review, such as *The Christian Florist*, *The History of Texas* and *Poetical Remains of the Late Lucretia Maria Davidson*. The answer to Auden is that Poe also wrote about Bryant, Byron,

Coleridge, Dickens, Hawthorne, Washington Irving, Longfellow, Shelley and Tennyson; a ninefold providing scope enough for any authentic critical consciousness. Nothing that Poe had to say about these poets and story-tellers is in any way memorable or at all an aid to reading them. There are no critical insights, no original perceptions, no accurate or illuminating juxtapositions or historical placements. Here is Poe on Tennyson, from his *Marginalia,* which generally surpass his other criticism:

> Why do some persons fatigue themselves in attempts to unravel such phantasy-pieces as the "Lady of Shalott"? . . . If the author did not deliberately propose to himself a suggestive indefinitiveness of meaning, with the view of bringing about a definitiveness of vague and therefore of spiritual *effect*—this, at least, arose from the silent analytical promptings of that poetic genius which, in its supreme development, embodies all orders of intellectual capacity.

I take this as being representative of Poe's criticism, because it is uninterestingly just plain *wrong* about "The Lady of Shalott." No other poem, even by the great word-painter Tennyson, is deliberately so definite in meaning and effect. Everything vague precisely is excluded in this perhaps most Pre-Raphaelite of all poems, where each detail contributes to an impression that might be called hard-edged phantasmagoria. If we take as the three possibilities of nineteenth century practical criticism the sequence of Arnold, Pater and Wilde, we find Poe useless in all three modes: Arnold's seeing the object as in itself it really is, Pater's seeing accurately one's own impression of the object, and the divine Oscar's sublime seeing of the object as in itself it really is not. If "The Lady of Shalott" is the object, then Poe does not see anything: the poem as in itself it is, one's impression of the poem as that is, or best of all the Wildean sense of what is missing or excluded from the poem. Poe's descriptive terms are "indefinitiveness" and "vague," but Tennyson's poem is just the reverse:

> She left the web, she left the loom,
> She made three paces through the room,
> She saw the water-lily bloom,
> She saw the helmet and the plume,
>   She looked down to Camelot.
> Out flew the web and floated wide;
> The mirror cracked from side to side;
> "The curse is come upon me," cried
>   The Lady of Shalott.

No, Poe as practical critic is a true match for most of his contemporary subjects, such as S. Anna Lewis, author of *The Child of the Sea and other Poems* (1848). Of her lyric, "The Forsaken," Poe wrote: "We have read this little poem more than twenty times and always with increasing admiration. *It is inexpressibly beautiful*" (Poe's italics). I quote only the first of its six stanzas:

It hath been said—for all who die
there is a tear;
Some pining, bleeding heart to sigh
O'er every bier:
But in that hour of pain and dread
Who will draw near
Around my humble couch and shed
One farewell tear?

Well, but there is Poe as theoretician, Valéry has told us. Acute self-consciousness in Poe was strongly misread by Valéry as the inauguration and development of severe and skeptical ideas. Presumably, this is the Poe of three famous essays: "The Philosophy of Composition," "The Rationale of Verse," and "The Poetic Principle." Having just reread these pieces, I have no possibility of understanding a letter of Valéry to Mallarmé which prizes the theories of Poe as being "so profound and so insidiously learned." Certainly we prize the theories of Valéry for just those qualities, and so I have come full circle to where I began, with the mystery of French Poe. Valéry may be said to have read Poe in the critical modes both of Pater and of Wilde. He saw his impression of Poe clearly, and he saw Poe's essays as in themselves they really were not. Admirable, and so Valéry brought to culmination the critical myth that is French Poe.

VII

Whose head is swinging from the swollen strap?
Whose body smokes along the bitten rails,
Bursts from a smoldering bundle far behind
In back forks of the chasms of the brain,—
Puffs from a riven stump far out behind
In interborough fissures of the mind . . . ?

Hart Crane's vision of Poe, in "The Tunnel" section of *The Bridge*, tells us again why the mythopoeic Poe is inescapable for American literary mythology. Poe's nightmare projections and introjections suggest the New York City subway as the new underground, where Coleridge's "deep Romantic chasm" has been internalized into "the chasms of the brain." Whatever his actual failures as poet and critic, whatever the gap between style and idea in his tales, Poe is central to the American canon, both for us and for the rest of the world. Hawthorne implicitly and Melville explicitly made far more powerful critiques of the Emersonian national hope, but they were by no means wholly negative in regard to Emerson and his pragmatic vision of

American Self-Reliance. Poe was savage in denouncing minor transcendentalists like Bronson Alcott and William Ellery Channing, but his explicit rejection of Emerson confined itself to the untruthful observation that Emerson was indistinguishable from Thomas Carlyle. Poe should have survived to read Carlyle's insane and amazing pamphlet on "The Nigger Question," which he would have adored. Mythologically, Poe is necessary because all of his work is a hymn to negativity. Emerson was a great theoretician of literature as of life, a good practical critic (when he wanted to be, which was not often), a very good poet (sometimes) and always a major aphorist and essayist. Poe, on a line-by-line or sentence-by-sentence basis, is hardly a worthy opponent. But looking in the French way, as T.S. Eliot recommended: "we see a mass of unique shape and impressive size to which the eye constantly returns." Eliot was probably right, in mythopoeic terms.

PAUL VALÉRY

On Poe's "Eureka"

I was twenty and believed in majesty of thought. I found it a strange torture to be, and not to be. At times I could feel infinite forces within me. They disappeared when faced with problems, and the weakness of my effective powers filled me with despair. I was moody, quick, tolerant in appearance, fundamentally hard, extreme in contempt, absolute in admiration, easy to impress, impossible to convince. I put my faith in a few ideas which had come to me. I regarded their conformity with the being which gave them birth as a certain indication of their universal value. Since they appeared so distinctly to my mind, they also appeared invincible; convictions born of desire are always the strongest.

I guarded these shadowy ideas as my secrets of state. I was ashamed of their strangeness; I feared they were absurd; I even knew they were absurd, but not entirely so. They were vain in themselves, but powerful by virtue of the remarkable force with which my confidence endowed me. My jealous watch over this mystery of weakness filled me with a sort of vigour.

I had ceased to write verse, and had almost ceased to read. Novels and poems, in my opinion, were only impure and half-unconscious applications of a few properties inherent in the great secrets I hoped some day to reveal—basing this hope on the unremitting assurance that they must necessarily exist. As for philosophers, I had read them very little, and was irritated by that little, because they never answered any of the questions which tormented me. They filled me only with boredom; never with the feeling that they were communicating some verifiable power. I thought it useless, moreover, to speculate about abstractions without first defining them. And yet can one do otherwise? The only hope for a philosophy is to render itself impersonal. We must await this great step toward the time of the world's end.

From *Variety* 1, translated by Malcolm Cowley. Copyright © 1927 by Harcourt Brace Jovanovich, Inc.

I had dipped into a few mystics. It is impossible to speak ill of their works, for all one discovers there is what one brings.

I was at this point when *Eureka* fell into my hands.

My studies under my dull and woebegone professors had led me to believe that science is not love; that its fruits are perhaps useful, but its foliage very spiny and its bark terribly rough. I reserved mathematics for a type of boringly exact minds, incommensurable with my own.

Literature, on the other hand, had often shocked me by its lack of discipline, connexion, and necessity in handling ideas. Frequently its object is trifling. French poetry ignores, or even fears, all the tragedies and epics of the intellect. On the few occasions when it ventures into this territory, it becomes sad and dull beyond measure. Neither Lucretius nor Dante was French. We have no poets of the intelligence. Perhaps our feeling for the separation of literary *genres*—in other words, for the independence of the different movements of the mind—is such that we can suffer nothing which combines them. Those things which can exist without singing we cannot endow with song. But our poetry, during the last hundred years, has shown such a rare power of renewal that perhaps the future will not be slow to grant it some of those works which are grand in their style, noble in their severity, and dominate both the senses and the intellect.

In a few moments *Eureka* had introduced me to Newton's law, the name of Laplace, the hypothesis which he proposed, and the very existence of speculations and researches which were never mentioned to adolescents—for fear, I suppose, that we might be interested, instead of measuring the astonishing length of the hour with yawns and dreams. In those days, whatever was likely to stimulate the intellectual appetite was placed among the arcana. It was a time when fat textbooks of physics did not whisper a word about the law of gravity, or Carnot's principle, or the conservation of energy; instead they were addicted to Magdeburg hemispheres, three-branched faucets, and the tenuous theories to which they were laboriously inspired by the problem of the siphon.

And yet, would it be wasting the time to study to make young minds suspect the origins, high destinies, and living virtue of those computations and very arid theorems which pedagogues inflict on them without logical order, and even with a rather remarkable incoherence?

These sciences now taught so coldly were founded and developed by men with a passionate interest in their work. *Eureka* made me feel some of this passion.

I confess that I was greatly astonished and only partially pleased by the preposterous claims and ambitions of the author, the solemn tone of his preamble, and the extraordinary discussion of method with which the volume opens. These first pages, however, gave indication of a central idea, although it was enveloped in a mystery which suggested partly a certain powerlessness, partly a deliberate reserve, and partly the reluctance of an enthusiastic soul to reveal its most precious secrets. . . . And all this did not leave me cold.

To attain what he calls *the truth*, Poe invokes what he calls *consistency*. It is not easy to give an exact definition of this consistency. The author has not done so, although he must have had a clear conception of its meaning.

According to him, the *truth* which he seeks can only be grasped by immediate adherence to an intuition of such nature that it renders present, and in some sort perceptible to the mind, the reciprocal dependence of the parts and properties of the system under consideration. This reciprocal dependence extends to the successive phases of the system; causality becomes symmetrical. To a point of view which embraced the totality of the universe, a cause and its effect might be taken one for the other; they could be said to exchange their rôles.

Two remarks at this point. The first I shall merely indicate, for it would lead us far, both the reader and myself. The doctrine of final causes plays a capital part in Poe's system. This doctrine is no longer fashionable, and I have neither the strength nor the desire to defend it. But we must agree that the notions of cause and adaptation lead almost inevitably to this conclusion (and I do not speak of the immense difficulties, and hence of the temptations, offered by certain facts, such as the existence of instincts, etc.). The simplest course is to dismiss the problem. Our only way of solving it is through pure imagination, and this can better be applied to other tasks.

Let us pass to the second remark. In Poe's system, consistency is both the source of the discovery and the discovery itself. This is an admirable conception: an example and application of reciprocal adaptation. The universe is formed on a plan the profound symmetry of which is present, as it were, in the inner structure of our minds. Hence, the poetic instinct will lead us blindly to the truth.

One frequently meets with analogous ideas among the mathematicians. They come to regard their discoveries not as "creations" of their mathematical faculties, but rather as something captured from a treasure composed of pre-existent and natural forms, a treasure which becomes accessible only through a rare conjecture of disciplined effort, sensibility, and desire.

All the consequences developed in *Eureka* are not deduced with the exactness, nor led up to with the degree of clarity, which one might desire. There are shadows and lacunae. There are interventions which the author hardly explains. There is a God.

For the spectator of the dramas and comedies of the intellect, nothing is more interesting than to see the ingenuity, the insistency, the trickery and anxiety of an inventor at grips with his own invention. He is admirably familiar with all its defects. He inevitably wishes to display all its beauties, exploit its advantages, conceal its poverty, and at any cost make it the image of his ideal. A merchant adorns his merchandise. A woman changes her appearance before a mirror. Preachers, philosophers, politicians, and, in general, all men whose function is to expound uncertain things, are always a mixture of sincerity and silences (and this is the most favourable assumption). What they do not wish to consider, they do not wish us to see. . . .

The fundamental idea of *Eureka* is none the less a profound and sovereign idea.

It would not be exaggerating its importance to recognize, in his theory of consistency, a fairly definite attempt to describe the universe by its *intrinsic properties.* The following proposition can be found toward the end of *Eureka*: "Each law of nature depends at all points on all the other laws." This might easily be considered, if not as a formula, at least as the expression of a tendency toward generalized relativity.

That this tendency approaches recent conceptions becomes evident when one discovers, in the *poem* under discussion, an affirmation of the *symmetrical* and reciprocal relationship of matter, time, space, gravity, and light. I emphasize the word symmetrical, for *it is, in reality, a formal symmetry which is the essential characteristic of Einstein's universe.* Herein lies the beauty of his conception.

But Poe does not confine himself to the physical constituents of phenomena. He introduces life and consciousness into his plan. At this point how many thoughts occur to the mind! The time is past when one could distinguish easily between the material and the spiritual. Formerly all discussion was based on a complete knowledge of "matter," which it was thought could be limited by definition. In a word, everything depended on *appearance.*

The appearance of matter is that of a dead substance, a *potentiality* which becomes *activity* only through the intervention of something exterior and entirely foreign to its nature. From this definition, inevitable consequences used to be drawn. But matter has changed. Our old conception of its nature was derived from pure observation; experiments have led to an opposite notion. The whole of modern physics, which has created, as it were, *relays* for our senses, has persuaded us that our former definition had neither an absolute nor a speculative value. We find that matter is strangely diverse and infinitely surprising; that it is formed of transformations which continue and are lost in minuteness, even in the abysses of minuteness; we learn that perpetual motion is perhaps realized. In matter an eternal fever rages.

At present we no longer know what a fragment of any given body may or may not contain or produce, now or in the future. The very idea of matter is distinguished as little as you will from that of energy. Everything is stirred by deeper and deeper agitations, rotations, exchanges, radiations. Our own eyes, our hands, our nerves, are made of such stuff; and the appearance of death or sleep which matter at first presents, as well as its passivity and surrender to external forces, are conceptions built up in our senses, like those shadows obtained by a certain superposition of lights.

All this can be resumed in the statement that the properties of matter seem to depend only on the category of size in which we place the observer. But in this case the classical attributes of matter—its lack of spontaneity, its essential difference from movement, and the continuity or homogeneity of its texture—become merely superficial, and can no longer be absolutely contrasted with such concepts as life, sensibility, or thought. Once we depart from the category of size in which rough observations are made, all former definitions prove incorrect. We are certain that unknown properties and forces are exerted in the *infra-world*, since we have discovered a few of these which our senses were not made to perceive. But we can neither enumerate them, nor even assign a definite number to the increasing plurality of chapters in the science of physics.

We cannot even be certain that the whole body of our concepts is not illusory, when transported into those domains which limit and support our own. To speak of iron or hydrogen is to presuppose entities—the existence and permanence of which can only be inferred from very limited and comparatively brief experiments. Moreover, there is no reason to believe that our space, our time, and our causality preserve any meaning whatsoever in those domains where the existence of our bodies is *impossible*. And certainly, the man who attempts to imagine the inner reality of things can do so only by adapting the ordinary categories of his mind. But the more he extends his researches, and, in some degree, the more he increases his powers of recording phenomena, the further he travels from what might be called the *optimum* of his perceptions. Determinism is lost among inextricable systems, with billions of variables, where the mind's eye can no longer trace the operation of laws and come to rest on some permanent fact. Whereas the imagination was once employed in giving final form to a truth which the senses had led one to infer, and the power of logic had woven into a single piece—now, when discontinuity becomes the rule, this imagination must confess its impotence. And when the *means* become the objects of our judgments, we are ceasing to consider events in themselves. Our knowledge is tending toward power, and has turned aside from a coordinated contemplation of things; prodigies of mathematical subtlety are required to restore a little unity to our world. We mention first principles no longer, and physical laws have become mere instruments, always capable of being perfected. They no longer govern the world, but are involved in the weakness of our minds; we can no longer rely on their simplicity; always, like a persistent point, there is some unresolved decimal which brings us back to a feeling of incompleteness, a sense of the inexhaustible.

One can see, from these remarks, that Poe's intuitions as to the general nature of the physical, moral, and metaphysical universe are neither proved nor disproved by the extremely numerous and important discoveries which have been made since 1847. Certain of his views could even be incorporated, without excessive difficulty, into fairly recent conceptions. When he measures the duration of his Cosmos by the time necessary to realize all possible combinations of the elements, one thinks of Boltzmann's theories and of his estimates of probability as applied to the kinetic theory of gas. Carnot's principle is also foreshadowed in *Eureka*, as is the representation of this principle by the mechanics of diffusion; the author seems to have been a precursor of those bold spirits who would rescue the universe from its certain death by means of an infinitely brief passage through an infinitely improbable state.

Since a complete analysis of *Eureka* is not my present intention, I shall hardly mention the use which Poe makes of the nebular hypothesis. When Laplace advanced this theory, his object was limited. He proposed only to reconstruct the development of the solar system. To this end he assumed the existence of a gaseous mass in the process of cooling. The core of the mass had already reached a high degree of condensation, and the whole rotated on an axis passing through its centre of gravity. He assumed the existence of this gravity, as well as the invariability of mechanical laws, and made it his sole task to explain the direction of rotation of the planets and their satellites, the slight eccentricity of their orbits, and the relatively small degree of inclination. Under these conditions, being subjected to centrifugal force and the process of cooling, matter would flow from the poles toward the equator of the mass, and at the points where gravity and centrifugal acceleration balanced each other, would be disposed in a zone. Thus a nebulous ring was formed; it would soon be broken, and the fragments of this ring would finally coalesce to form a planet.

The reader of *Eureka* will see how Poe has extended the application both of the nebular hypothesis and the law of gravity. On these mathematical foundations he has built an abstract poem, one of the rare modern examples of a total explanation of the material and spiritual universe, a *cosmogony*. It belongs to a department of literature remarkable for its persistence and astonishing in its variety; cosmogony is one of the oldest of all literary forms.

DAVID HERBERT LAWRENCE

Edgar Allan Poe

Poe has no truck with Indians or Nature. He makes no bones about Red Brothers and Wigwams.

He is absolutely concerned with the disintegration-processes of his own psyche. As we have said, the rhythm of American art-activity is dual.

1. A disintegrating and sloughing of the old consciousness.

2. The forming of a new consciousness underneath.

Fenimore Cooper has the two vibrations going on together. Poe has only one, only the disintegrative vibration. This makes him almost more a scientist than an artist.

Moralists have always wondered helplessly why Poe's "morbid" tales need have been written. They need to be written because old things need to die and disintegrate, because the old white psyche has to be gradually broken down before anything else can come to pass.

Man must be stripped even of himself. And it is a painful, sometimes a ghastly, process.

Poe had a pretty bitter doom. Doomed to seethe down his soul in a great continuous convulsion of disintegration, and doomed to register the process. And then doomed to be abused for it, when he had performed some of the bitterest tasks of human experience, that can be asked of a man. Necessary tasks, too. For the human soul must suffer its own disintegration, *consciously*, if ever it is to survive.

But Poe is rather a scientist than an artist. He is reducing his own self as a scientist reduces a salt in a crucible. It is an almost chemical analysis of the soul and consciousness. Whereas in true art there is always the double rhythm of creating and destroying.

This is why Poe calls his things "tales." They are a concatenation of cause and effect.

From *Studies in Classic American Literature.* Copyright © 1923 by The Viking Press.

His best pieces, however, are not tales. They are more. They are ghastly stories of the human soul in its disruptive throes.

Moreover, they are "love" stories.

Ligeia and *The Fall of the House of Usher* are really love stories.

Love is the mysterious vital attraction which draws things together, closer, closer together. For this reason sex is the actual crisis of love. For in sex the two blood-systems, in the male and female, concentrate and come into contact, the merest film intervening. Yet if the intervening film breaks down, it is death.

So there you are. There is a limit to everything. There is a limit to love.

The central law of all organic life is that each organism is intrinsically isolate and single in itself.

The moment its isolation breaks down, and there comes an actual mixing and confusion, death sets in.

This is true of every individual organism, from man to amoeba.

But the secondary law of all organic life is that each organism only lives through contact with other matter, assimilation, and contact with other life, which means assimilation of new vibrations, nonmaterial. Each individual organism is vivified by intimate contact with fellow organisms: up to a certain point.

So man. He breathes the air into him, he swallows food and water. But more than this. He takes into him the life of his fellow men, with whom he comes into contact, and he gives back life to them. This contact draws nearer and nearer, as the intimacy increases. When it is a whole contact, we call it love. Men live by food, but die if they eat too much. Men live by love, but die, or cause death, if they love too much.

There are two loves: sacred and profane, spiritual and sensual.

In sensual love, it is the two blood-systems, the man's and the woman's, which sweep up into pure contact, and *almost* fuse. Almost mingle. Never quite. There is always the finest imaginable wall between the two blood-waves, through which pass unknown vibrations, forces, but through which the blood itself must never break, or it means bleeding.

In spiritual love, the contact is purely nervous. The nerves in the lovers are set vibrating in unison like two instruments. The pitch can rise higher and higher. But carry this too far, and the nerves begin to break, to bleed, as it were, and a form of death sets in.

The trouble about man is that he insists on being master of his own fate, and he insists on *oneness*. For instance, having discovered the ecstasy of spiritual love, he insists that he shall have this all the time, and nothing but this, for this is life. It is what he calls "heightening" life. He wants his nerves to be set vibrating in the intense and exhilarating unison with the nerves of another being, and by this means he acquires an ecstasy of vision, he finds himself in glowing unison with all the universe.

But as a matter of fact this glowing unison is only a temporary thing, because the first law of life is that each organism is isolate in itself, it must return to its own isolation.

Yet man has tried the glow of unison, called love, and he *likes* it. It gives him his highest gratification. He wants it. He wants it all the time. He wants it and he will have it. He doesn't want to return to his own isolation. Or if he must, it is only as a prowling beast returns to its lair to rest and set out again.

This brings us to Edgar Allan Poe. The clue to him lies in the motto he chose for *Ligeia*, a quotation from the mystic Joseph Glanvill: "And the will therein lieth, which dieth not. Who knoweth the mysteries of the will, with its vigour? For God is but a great will pervading all things by nature of its intentness. Man doth not yield himself to the angels, nor unto death utterly, save only through the weakness of his feeble will."

It is a profound saying: and a deadly one.

Because if God is a great will, then the universe is but an instrument.

I don't know what God is. But He is not simply a will. That is too simple. Too anthropomorphic. Because a man wants his own will, and nothing but his will, he needn't say that God is the same will, magnified *ad infinitum.*

For me, there may be one God, but He is nameless and unknowable.

For me, there are also many gods, that come into me and leave me again. And they have very various wills, I must say.

But the point is Poe.

Poe had experienced the ecstasies of extreme spiritual love. And he wanted those ecstasies and nothing but those ecstasies. He wanted that great gratification, the sense of flowing, the sense of unison, the sense of heightening of life. He had experienced this gratification. He was told on every hand that this ecstasy of spiritual, nervous love was the greatest thing in life, was life itself. And he had tried it for himself, he knew that for him it *was* life itself. So he wanted it. And he *would have* it. He set up his will against the whole of the limitations of nature.

This is a brave man, acting on his own belief, and his own experience. But it is also an arrogant man, and a fool.

Poe was going to get the ecstasy and the heightening, cost what it might. He went on in a frenzy, as characteristic American women nowadays go on in a frenzy, after the very same thing: the heightening, the flow, the ecstasy. Poe tried alcohol, and any drug he could lay his hands on. He also tried any human being he could lay his hands on.

His grand attempt and achievement was with his wife; his cousin, a girl with a singing voice. With her he went in for the intensest flow, the heightening, the prismatic shades of ecstasy. It was the intensest nervous vibration of unison, pressed higher and higher in pitch, till the blood-vessels of the girl broke, and the blood began to flow out loose. It was love. If you call it love.

Love can be terribly obscene.

It is love that causes the neuroticism of the day. It is love that is the prime cause of tuberculosis.

The nerves that vibrate most intensely in spiritual unisons are the sympathetic ganglia of the breast, of the throat, and the hind brain. Drive this vibration over-intensely, and you weaken the sympathetic tissues of the chest—the lungs—or of the throat, or of the lower brain, and the tubercles are given a ripe field.

But Poe drove the vibrations beyond any human pitch of endurance.

Being his cousin, she was more easily keyed to him.

Ligeia is the chief story. Ligeia! A mental-derived name. To him the woman, his wife, was not Lucy. She was Ligeia. No doubt she even preferred it thus.

Ligeia is Poe's love-story, and its very fantasy makes it more truly his own story.

It is a tale of love pushed over a verge. And love pushed to extremes is a battle of wills between the lovers.

Love is become a battle of wills.

Which shall first destroy the other, of the lovers? Which can hold out longest, against the other?

Ligeia is still the old-fashioned woman. Her will is still to submit. She wills to submit to the vampire of her husband's consciousness. Even death.

"In stature she was tall, somewhat slender, and, in her latter days, even emaciated. I would in vain attempt to portray the majesty, the quiet ease, of her demeanour, or the incomprehensible lightness and elasticity of her footfall. . . . I was never made aware of her entrance into my closed study, save by the dear music of her low sweet voice, as she placed her marble hand upon my shoulder."

Poe has been so praised for his style. But it seems to me a meretricious affair. "Her marble hand" and "the elasticity of her footfall" seem more like chair-springs and mantelpieces than a human creature. She never was quite a human creature to him. She was an instrument from which he got his extremes of sensation. His *machine à plaisir*, as somebody says.

All Poe's style, moreover, has this mechanical quality, as his poetry has a mechanical rhythm. He never sees anything in terms of life, almost always in terms of matter, jewels, marble, etc.,—or in terms of force, scientific. And his cadences are all managed mechanically. This is what is called "having a style."

What he wants to do with Ligeia is to analyse her, till he knows all her component parts, till he has got her all in his consciousness. She is some strange chemical salt which he must analyse out in the test-tubes of his brain, and then—when he's finished the analysis—*E finita la commedia!*

But she won't be quite analysed out. There is something, something he can't get. Writing of her eyes, he says: "They were, I must believe, far larger than the ordinary eyes of our own race"—as if anybody would want eyes "far larger" than other folks'. "They were even fuller than the fullest of the gazelle eyes of the tribe of the valley of Nourjahad"—which is blarney. "The hue of the orbs was the most brilliant of black and, far over them, hung jetty lashes of great length"—suggests a whiplash. "The brows, slightly irregular in outline, had the same tint. The 'strangeness,' however, which I found in the eyes, was of a nature distinct from the formation, or the colour, or the brilliancy of the features, and must, after all, be referred to the *expression.*"— Sounds like an anatomist anatomizing a cat—"Ah, word of no meaning! behind whose vast latitude of mere sound we entrench our ignorance of so much of the spiritual. The expression of the eyes of Ligeia! How for long hours have I pondered upon it! How have I, through the whole of a mid-summer night, struggled to fathom it! What was it—that something more profound than the well of Democritus—which lay far within the pupils of my beloved! What *was* it? I was possessed with a passion to discover. . . ."

It is easy to see why each man kills the thing he loves. To *know* a living thing is to kill it. You have to kill a thing to know it satisfactorily. For this reason, the desirous consciousness, the SPIRIT, is a vampire.

One should be sufficiently intelligent and interested to know a good deal *about* any person one comes into close contact with. *About* her. Or *about* him.

But to try to *know* any living being is to try to suck the life out of that being.

Above all things, with the woman one loves. Every sacred instinct teaches one that one must leave her unknown. You know your woman darkly, in the blood. To try to *know* her mentally is to try to kill her. Beware, oh woman, of the man who wants to *find out what you are.* And, oh men, beware a thousand times more of the woman who wants to *know* you, or *get* you, what you are.

It is the temptation of a vampire fiend, is this knowledge.

Man does so horribly want to master the secret of life and of individuality *with his mind.* It is like the analysis of protoplasm. You can only analyse *dead* protoplasm, and know its constituents. It is a death-process.

Keep KNOWLEDGE for the world of matter, force, and function. It has got nothing to do with being.

But Poe wanted to know—wanted to know what was the strangeness in the eyes of Ligeia. She might have told him it was horror at his probing, horror at being vamped by his consciousness.

But she wanted to be vamped. She wanted to be probed by his consciousness, to be KNOWN. She paid for wanting it, too.

Nowadays it is usually the man who wants to be vamped, to be KNOWN.

Edgar Allan probed and probed. So often he seemed on the verge. But she went over the verge of death before he came over the verge of knowledge. And it is always so.

He decided, therefore, that the clue to the strangeness lay in the mystery of will. "And the will therein lieth, which dieth not . . ."

Ligeia had a "gigantic volition." . . . "An intensity in thought, action, or speech was possibly, in her, a result, or at least an index" (he really meant indication) "of that gigantic volition which, during our long intercourse, failed to give other and more immediate evidence of its existence."

I should have thought her long submission to him was chief and ample "other evidence."

"Of all the women whom I have ever known, she, the outwardly calm, ever-placid Ligeia, was the most violently a prey to the tumultuous vultures of stern passion. And of such passion I could form no estimate, save by the miraculous expansion of those eyes which at once so delighted and appalled me—by the almost magical melody, modulation, distinctness, and placidity of her very low voice—and by the fierce energy (rendered doubly effective by contrast with her manner of utterance) of the wild words which she habitually uttered."

Poor Poe, he had caught a bird of the same feather as himself. One of those terrible cravers, who crave the further sensation. Crave to madness or death. "Vultures of stern passion" indeed! Condors.

But having recognized that the clue was in her gigantic volition, he should have realized that the process of this loving, this craving, this knowing, was a struggle of wills. But Ligeia, true to the great tradition and mode of womanly love, by her will kept herself submissive, recipient. She is the passive body who is explored and analysed into death. And yet, at times, her great female will must have revolted. "Vultures of stern passion!" With a convulsion of desire she desired his further probing and exploring. To any lengths. But then, "tumultuous vultures of stern passion." She had to fight with herself.

But Ligeia wanted to go on and on with the craving, with the love, with the sensation, with the probing, with the knowing, on and on to the end.

There is no end. There is only the rupture of death. That's where men, and women, are "had." Man is always sold, in his search for final KNOWLEDGE.

"That she loved me I should not have doubted; and I might have been easily aware that, in a bosom such as hers, love would have reigned no ordinary passion. But in death only was I fully impressed with the strength of her affection. For long hours, detaining my hand, would she pour out before me the overflowing of a heart whose more than passionate devotion amounted to idolatry." (Oh, the indecency of all this endless intimate talk!) "How had I deserved to be so blessed by such confessions?" (Another man would have felt himself cursed.) "How had I deserved to be so cursed with the removal of my beloved in the hour of her making them? But upon this subject I cannot bear to dilate. Let me say only that in Ligeia's more than womanly abandonment to a love, alas! all unmerited, all unworthily bestowed, I at length recognized the principle of her longing, with so wildly earnest a desire, for the life which was now fleeing so rapidly away. It is this wild longing—it is this eager vehemence of desire for life—*but* for life, that I have no power to portray, no utterance capable of expressing."

Well, that is ghastly enough, in all conscience.

"And from them that have not shall be taken away even that which they have."

"To him that hath life shall be given life, and from him that hath not life shall be taken away even that life which he hath."

Or her either.

These terribly conscious birds, like Poe and his Ligeia, deny the very life that is in them; they want to turn it all into talk, into *knowing*. And so life, which will *not* be known, leaves them.

But poor Ligeia, how could she help it? It was her doom. All the centuries of the SPIRIT, all the years of American rebellion against the Holy Ghost, had done it to her.

She dies, when she would rather do anything than die. And when she dies the clue, which he only lived to grasp, dies with her.

Foiled!

Foiled!

No wonder she shrieks with her last breath.

On the last day Ligeia dictates to her husband a poem. As poems go, it is rather false, meretricious. But put yourself in Ligeia's place, and it is real enough, and ghastly beyond bearing.

> Out—out are all the lights—out all!
> 　　And over each quivering form
> The curtain, a funeral pall,
> 　　Comes down with the rush of a storm,
> While the angels, all pallid and wan,
> 　　Uprising, unveiling, affirm
> That the play is the tragedy, 'Man,'
> 　　And its hero, the Conqueror Worm.

Which is the American equivalent for a William Blake poem. For Blake, too, was one of these ghastly, obscene "Knowers."

" 'O God!' half shrieked Ligeia leaping to her feet and extending her arms aloft with a spasmodic movement, as I made an end of these lines—'O God! O Divine Father! shall these things be undeviatingly so? Shall this conqueror be not once conquered? Are we not part and parcel in Thee? Who—who knoweth the mysteries of the will with its vigour? Man doth not yield him to the angels, *nor unto death utterly*, save only through the weakness of his feeble will.' "

So Ligeia dies. And yields to death at least partly. *Anche troppo.*

As for her cry to God—has not God said that those who sin against the Holy Ghost shall not be forgiven?

And the Holy Ghost is within us. It is the thing that prompts us to be real, not to push our own cravings too far, not to submit to stunts and high-falutin, above all, not to be too egoistic and wilful in our conscious self, but to change as the spirit inside us bids us change, and leave off when it bids us leave off, and laugh when we must laugh, particularly at ourselves, for in deadly earnestness there is always something a bit ridiculous. The Holy Ghost bids us never be too deadly in our earnestness, always to laugh in time, at ourselves and everything. Particularly at our sublimities. Everything has its hour of ridicule—everything.

Now Poe and Ligeia, alas, couldn't laugh. They were frenziedly earnest. And frenziedly they pushed on this vibration of consciousness and unison in consciousness. They sinned against the Holy Ghost that bids us all laugh and forget, bids us know our own limits. And they weren't forgiven.

Ligeia needn't blame God. She had only her own will, her "gigantic volition" to thank, lusting after more consciousness, more beastly KNOWING.

Ligeia dies. The husband goes to England, vulgarly buys or rents a gloomy, grand old abbey, puts it into some sort of repair, and furnishes it with exotic, mysterious, theatrical splendour. Never anything open and real. This theatrical "volition" of his. The bad taste of sensationalism.

Then he marries the fair-haired, blue-eyed Lady Rowena Trevanion, of Tremaine. That is, she would be a sort of Saxon-Cornish blue-blood damsel. Poor Poe!

"In halls such as these—in a bridal chamber such as this—I passed, with the Lady of Tremaine, the unhallowed hours of the first month of our marriage—passed them with but little disquietude. That my wife dreaded the fierce moodiness of my temper—that she shunned me and loved me but little—I could not help perceiving, but it gave me rather pleasure than otherwise. I loathed her with a hatred belonging more to demon than to man. My memory flew back (oh, with what intensity of regret!) to Ligeia, the beloved, the august, the beautiful, the entombed. I revelled in recollections of her purity . . ." etc.

Now the vampire lust is consciously such.

In the second month of the marriage the Lady Rowena fell ill. It is the shadow of Ligeia hangs over her. It is the ghostly Ligeia who pours poison into Rowena's cup. It is the spirit of Ligeia, leagued with the spirit of the husband, that now lusts in the slow destruction of Rowena. The two vampires, dead wife and living husband.

For Ligeia has not yielded unto death *utterly*. Her fixed, frustrated will comes back in vindictiveness. She could not have her way in life. So she, too, will find victims in life. And the husband, all the time, only uses Rowena as a living body on which to wreak his vengeance for his being thwarted with Ligeia. Thwarted from the final KNOWING her.

And at last from the corpse of Rowena, Ligeia rises. Out of her death, through the door of a corpse they have destroyed between them, reappears Ligeia, still trying to have her will, to have more love and knowledge, the final gratification which is never final, with her husband.

For it is true, as William James and Conan Doyle and the rest allow, that a spirit can persist in the after-death. Persist by its own volition. But usually, the evil persistence of a thwarted will, returning for vengeance on life. Lemures, vampires.

It is a ghastly story of the assertion of the human will, the will-to-love and the will-to-consciousness, asserted against death itself. The pride of human conceit in KNOWLEDGE.

There are terrible spirits, ghosts, in the air of America.

Eleanora, the next story, is a fantasy revealing the sensational delights of the man in his early marriage with the young and tender bride. They dwelt, he, his cousin and her mother, in the sequestered Valley of Many-coloured Grass, the valley of prismatic sensation, where everything seems spectrum-coloured. They looked down at their *own images* in the River of Silence, and drew the god Eros from that wave: out of their own self-consciousness, that is. This is a description of the life of introspection and of the love which is begotten by the self in the self, the self-made love. The trees are like serpents worshipping the sun. That is, they represent the phallic passion in its poisonous or mental activity. Everything runs to consciousness: serpents worshipping the sun. The embrace of love, which should bring darkness and oblivion, would with these lovers be a daytime thing bringing more heightened consciousness, visions, spectrum-visions, prismatic. The evil thing that daytime love-making is, and all sex-palaver.

In *Berenice* the man must go down to the sepulchre of his beloved and pull out her thirty-two small white teeth, which he carries in a box with him. It is repulsive and gloating. The teeth are the instruments of biting, of resistance, of antagonism. They often become symbols of opposition, little instruments or entities of crushing and destroying. Hence the dragon's teeth in the myth. Hence the man in *Berenice* must take possession of the irreducible part of his mistress. "*Toutes ses dents étaient des idées,*" he says. Then they are little fixed ideas of mordant hate, of which he possesses himself.

The other great story linking up with this group is *The Fall of the House of Usher*. Here the love is between brother and sister. When the self is broken, and the mystery of the recognition of *otherness* fails, then the longing for identification with the beloved becomes a lust. And it is this longing for identification, utter merging, which is at the base of the incest problem. In psychoanalysis almost every trouble in the psyche is traced to an incest-desire. But it won't do. Incest-desire is only one of the modes by which men strive to get their gratification of the intensest vibration of the spiritual nerves, without any resistance. In the family, the natural vibration is most nearly in unison. With a stranger, there is greater resistance. Incest is the getting of gratification and the avoiding of resistance.

The root of all evil is that we all want this spiritual gratification, this flow, this apparent heightening of life, this knowledge, this valley of many-coloured grass, even grass and light prismatically decomposed, giving esctasy. We want all this *without resistance*. We want it continually. And this is the root of all evil in us.

We ought to pray to be resisted, and resisted to the bitter end. We ought to decide to have done at last with craving.

The motto to *The Fall of the House of Usher* is a couple of lines from Béranger.

> *Son coeur est un luth suspendu;*
> *Sitôt qu'on le touche il résonne.*

We have all the trappings of Poe's rather overdone, vulgar fantasy. "I reined my horse to the precipitous brink of a black and lurid tarn that lay in unruffled lustre by the dwelling, and gazed down—but with a shudder even more thrilling than before—upon the remodelled and inverted images of the grey sedge, and the ghastly tree-stems, and the vacant and eye-like windows." The House of Usher, both dwelling and family, was very old. Minute fungi overspread the exterior of the house, hanging in festoons from the eaves.

Gothic archways, a valet of stealthy step, sombre tapestries, ebon black floors, a profusion of tattered and antique furniture, feeble gleams of encrimsoned light through latticed panes, and over all "an air of stern, deep, and irredeemable gloom"—this makes up the interior.

The inmates of the house, Roderick and Madeline Usher, are the last remnants of their incomparably ancient and decayed race. Roderick has the same large, luminous eye, the same slightly arched nose of delicate Hebrew model, as characterized Ligeia. He is ill with the nervous malady of his family. It is he whose nerves are so strung that they vibrate to the unknown quiverings of the ether. He, too, has lost his self, his living soul, and becomes a sensitized instrument of the external influences; his nerves are verily like an aeolian harp which must vibrate. He lives in "some struggle with the grim phantasm, Fear," for he is only the physical, post-mortem reality of a living being.

It is a question how much, once the true centrality of the self is broken, the instrumental consciousness of man can register. When man becomes selfless, wafting instrumental like a harp in an open window, how much can his elemental consciousness express? The blood as it runs has its own sympathies and responses to the material world, quite apart from seeing. And the nerves we know vibrate all the while to unseen presences, unseen forces. So Roderick Usher quivers on the edge of material existence.

It is this mechanical consciousness which gives "the fervid facility of his impromptus." It is the same thing that gives Poe his extraordinary facility in versification. The absence of real central or impulsive being in himself leaves him inordinately, mechanically sensitive to sounds and effects, associations of sounds, associations of rhyme, for example—mechanical, facile, having no root in any passion. It is all a secondary, meretricious process. So we get Roderick Usher's poem, *The Haunted Palace*, with its swift yet mechanical subtleties of rhyme and rhythm, its vulgarity of epithet. It is all a sort of dream-process, where the association between parts is mechanical, accidental as far as passional meaning goes.

Usher thought that all vegetable things had sentience. Surely all material things have a *form* of sentience, even the inorganic: surely they all exist in some subtle and complicated tension of vibration which makes them sensitive to external influence and causes them to have an influence on other external objects, irrespective of contact. It is of this vibration or inorganic consciousness that Poe is master: the sleep-consciousness. Thus Roderick Usher was convinced that his whole surroundings, the stones of the house, the fungi, the water in the tarn, the very reflected image of the whole, was woven into a physical oneness with the family, condensed, as it were, into one atmosphere—the special atmosphere in which alone the Ushers could live. And it was this atmosphere which had moulded the destinies of his family.

But while ever the soul remains alive, it is the moulder and not the moulded. It is the souls of living men that subtly impregnate stones, houses, mountains, continents, and give these their subtlest form. People only become subject to stones after having lost their integral souls.

In the human realm, Roderick had one connection: his sister Madeline. She, too, was dying of a mysterious disorder, nervous, cataleptic. The brother and sister loved each other passionately and exclusively. They were twins, almost identical in looks. It was the same absorbing love between them, this process of unison in nerve-vibration, resulting in more and more extreme exaltation and a sort of consciousness, and a gradual breakdown into death. The exquisitely sensitive Roger, vibrating without resistance with his sister Madeline, more and more exquisitely, and gradually devouring her, sucking her life like a vampire in his anguish of extreme love. And she asking to be sucked.

Madeline died and was carried down by her brother into the deep vaults of the house. But she was not dead. Her brother roamed about in incipient madness—a madness of unspeakable terror and guilt. After eight days they were suddenly startled by a clash of metal, then a distinct, hollow metallic, and clangorous, yet apparently muffled, reverberation. Then Roderick Usher, gibbering, began to express himself: "*We have put her living in the tomb!* Said I not that my senses were acute! I *now* tell you that I heard her first feeble movements in the hollow coffin. I heard them—many, many days ago—yet I dared not—*I dared not speak.*"

It is the same old theme of "each man kills the thing he loves." He knew his love had killed her. He knew she died at last, like Ligeia, unwilling and unappeased. So, she rose again upon him. "But then without those doors there *did* stand the lofty and enshrouded figure of the lady Madeline of Usher. There was blood upon her white robes, and the evidence of some bitter struggle upon every portion of her emaciated frame. For a moment she remained trembling and reeling to and fro upon the threshold, then, with a low moaning cry, fell heavily inward upon the person of her brother, and in her violent and now final death-agonies bore him to the floor a corpse, and a victim to the terrors he had anticipated."

It is lurid and melodramatic, but it is true. It is a ghastly psychological truth of what happens in the last stages of this beloved love, which cannot be separate, cannot be isolate, cannot listen in isolation to the isolate Holy Ghost. For it is the Holy Ghost we must live by. The next era is the era of the Holy Ghost. And the Holy Ghost speaks individually inside each individual: always, forever a ghost. There is no manifestation to the general world. Each isolate individual listening in isolation to the Holy Ghost within him.

The Ushers, brother and sister, betrayed the Holy Ghost in themselves. They would love, love, love, without resistance. They would love, they would merge, they would be as one thing. So they dragged each other down into death. For the Holy Ghost says you must *not* be as one thing with another being. Each must abide by itself, and correspond only within certain limits.

The best tales all have the same burden. Hate is as inordinate as love, and as slowly consuming, as secret, as underground, as subtle. All this underground vault business in Poe only symbolizes that which takes place *beneath* the consciousness. On top, all is fair-spoken. Beneath, there is awful murderous extremity of burying alive. Fortunato, in *The Cask of Amontillado*, is buried alive out of perfect hatred, as the lady Madeline of Usher is buried alive out of love. The lust of hate is the inordinate desire to consume and unspeakably possess the soul of the hated one, just as the lust of love is the desire to possess, or to be possessed by, the beloved, utterly. But in either case the result is the dissolution of both souls, each losing itself in transgressing its own bounds.

The lust of Montresor is to devour utterly the soul of Fortunato. It would be no use killing him outright. If a man is killed outright his soul remains integral, free to return into the bosom of some beloved, where it can enact itself. In walling-up his enemy in the vault, Montresor seeks to bring about the indescribable capitulation of the man's soul, so that he, the victor, can possess himself of the very being of the vanquished. Perhaps this can actually be done. Perhaps, in the attempt, the victor breaks the bonds of his own identity, and collapses into nothingness, or into the infinite. Becomes a monster.

What holds good for inordinate hate holds good for inordinate love. The motto, *Nemo me impune lacessit*, might just as well be *Nemo me impune amat*.

In *William Wilson* we are given a rather unsubtle account of the attempt of a man to kill his own soul. William Wilson the mechanical, lustful ego succeeds in killing William Wilson the living self. The lustful ego lives on, gradually reducing itself towards the dust of the infinite.

In the *Murders in the Rue Morgue* and *The Gold Bug* we have those mechanical tales where the interest lies in the following out of a subtle chain of cause and effect. The interest is scientific rather than artistic, a study in psychologic reactions.

The fascination of murder itself is curious. Murder is not just killing. Murder is a lust to get at the very quick of life itself, and kill it—hence the stealth and the frequent morbid dismemberment of the corpse, the attempt to get at the very quick of the murdered being, to find the quick and to possess it. It is curious that the two men fascinated by the art of murder, though in different ways, should have been De Quincey and Poe, men so different in ways of life, yet perhaps not so widely different in nature. In each of them is traceable that strange lust for extreme love and extreme hate, possession by mystic violence of the other soul, or violent deathly surrender of the soul in the self: an absence of manly virtue, which stands alone and accepts limits.

Inquisition and torture are akin to murder: the same lust. It is a combat between inquisitor and victim as to whether the inquisitor shall get at the quick of life itself, and pierce it. Pierce the very quick of the soul. The evil will of man tries to do this. The brave soul of man refuses to have the life-quick pierced in him. It is strange: but just as the thwarted will can persist evilly, after death, so can the brave spirit preserve, even through torture and death, the quick of life and truth. Nowadays society is evil. It finds subtle ways of torture, to destroy the life-quick, to get at the life-quick in a man. Every possible form. And still a man can hold out, if he can laugh and listen to the Holy Ghost.—But society is evil, evil, and love is evil. And evil breeds evil, more and more.

So the mystery goes on. La Bruyère says that all our human unhappiness *viennent de ne pouvoir être seuls.* As long as man lives he will be subject to the yearning of love or the burning of hate, which is only inverted love.

But he is subject to something more than this. If we do not live to eat, we do not live to love either.

We live to stand alone, and listen to the Holy Ghost. The Holy Ghost, who is inside us, and who is many gods. Many gods come and go, some say one thing and some say another, and we have to obey the God of the innermost hour. It is the multiplicity of gods within us make up the Holy Ghost.

But Poe knew only love, love, intense vibrations and heightened consciousness. Drugs, women, self-destruction, but anyhow the prismatic ecstasy of heightened consciousness and sense of love, of flow. The human soul in him was beside itself. But it was not lost. He told us plainly how it was, so that we should know.

He was an adventurer into vaults and cellars and horrible underground passages of the human soul. He sounded the horror and the warning of his own doom.

Doomed he was. He died wanting more love, and love killed him. A ghastly disease, love. Poe telling us of his disease: trying even to make his disease fair and attractive. Even succeeding.

Which is the inevitable falseness, duplicity of art, American art in particular.

ALLEN TATE

The Angelic Imagination

With some embarrassment I assume
the part of amateur theologian and turn to a little-known figure, Edgar
Allan Poe, another theologian only less ignorant than myself. How seriously
one must take either Poe or his present critic in this new role I prefer not
to be qualified to say. Poe will remain a man of letters—I had almost said
a poet—whose interest for us is in the best sense historical. He represents
that part of our experience which we are least able to face up to: the Dark
Night of Sense, the cloud hovering over that edge of the eye which is
turned to receive the effluvia of France, whence the literary power of his
influence reaches us today. In France, the literary power has been closely
studied; I shall not try to estimate it here. Poe's other power, that of the
melancholy, heroic life, one must likewise leave to others, those of one's
own compatriots who are not interested in literature. All readers of Poe,
of the work or of the life, and the rare reader of both, are peculiarly liable
to the vanity of discovery. I shall be concerned in the ensuing remarks
with what I think I have seen in Poe that nobody else has seen: this
undetected quality, or its remote source in Poe's feeling and thought, I
believe partly explains an engagement with him that men on both sides of
the Atlantic have acknowledged for more than a century.

It was recently acknowledged, with reservations, by Mr. T.S. Eliot,
whose estimate must be reckoned with: Poe, he tells us, won a great reputation in
Europe because the continental critics habitually view an author's work as a
whole; whereas English and American critics view each work separately and,
in the case of Poe, have been stopped by its defects. Mr. Eliot's essay is the first
attempt by an English-speaking critic to bring to Poe the continental ap-

proach and to form a general estimate. I quote from what I take to be Mr. Eliot's summary; Poe, he says,

> appears to yield himself completely to the idea of the moment: the effect is, that all his ideas seem to be entertained rather than believed. What is lacking is not brain-power, but that maturity of intellect which comes only with the maturing of the man as a whole, the development and coordination of his various emotions.

What I shall say towards the end of this essay I believe will show that Mr. Eliot is partly wrong, but that on the whole his estimate of Poe's immaturity is right. Does Poe merely "entertain" *all* his ideas? Perhaps all but one; but that one makes all the difference. Its special difference consists in his failure to see what the idea really was, so that he had perpetually to shift his ground—to "entertain," one after another, shabby rhetorics and fantasies that could never quite contain the one great idea. He was a religious man whose Christianity, for reasons that nobody knows anything about, had got short-circuited; he lived among fragments of provincial theologies, in the midst of which "coordination," for a man of his intensity, was difficult if not impossible. There is no evidence that Poe used the word coordination in the sense in which Mr. Eliot finds him deficient in it; but it is justly applied. I am nevertheless surprised that Mr. Eliot seems to assume that *coordination* of the "various emotions" is ever possible: the word gives the case away to Poe. It is a morally neutral term that Poe himself might have used, in his lifelong effort to impose upon experience a mechanical logic; possibly it came into modern literary psychology from analytic geometry. I take it that the word was not used, if in Mr. Eliot's sense it was known, when considerable numbers of persons were able to experience coordination. I suppose Mr. Eliot means by it a harmony of faculties among different orders of experience; and Poe's failure to harmonize himself cannot be denied.

The failure resulted in a hypertrophy of the three classical faculties: feeling, will, and intellect. The first . . . is the incapacity to represent the human condition in the central tradition of natural feeling. A nightmare of paranoia, schizophrenia, necrophilism, and vampirism supervenes, in which the natural affections are perverted by the will to destroy. Poe's heroines— Berenice, Ligeia, Madeline, Morella, with the curious exception of the abstemious Eleanora—are ill-disguised vampires; his heroes become necromancers (in the root meaning of the word) whose wills, like the heroines' wills, defy the term of life to keep them equivocally "alive." This primary failure in human feeling results in the loss of the entire natural order of experience.

The second hypertrophy is the thrust of the will beyond the human scale of action. The evidence of this is on nearly every page of Poe's serious prose fiction. Poe's readers, especially the young, like the quotation from Glanvill that appears as the epigraph to "Ligeia": "Man does not yield himself to the angels, nor unto Death utterly, save only through the weakness of his feeble will." It is the theme of the major stories. The hero professes an impossibly high love of the heroine that circumvents the body and moves in upon her spiritual essence. All this sounds high and noble, until we begin to look at it more narrowly, when we perceive that the ordinary carnal relationship between man and woman, however sinful, would be preferable to the mutual destruction of soul to which Poe's characters are committed. The carnal act, in which none of them seems to be interested, would witness a commitment to the order of nature, without which the higher knowledge is not possible to man. The Poe-hero tries in self-love to turn the soul of the heroine into something like a physical object which he can know in direct cognition and then possess.

Thus we get the third hypertrophy of a human faculty: the intellect moving in isolation from both love and the moral will, whereby it declares itself independent of the human situation in the quest of essential knowledge.

The three perversions necessarily act together, the action of one implying a deflection of the others. But the actual emphases that Poe gives the perversions are richer in philosophical implication than his psychoanalytic critics have been prepared to see. To these ingenious persons, Poe's works have almost no intrinsic meaning; taken together they make up a *dossier* for the analyst to peruse before Mr. Poe steps into his office for an analysis. It is important at this point to observe that Poe takes for granted the old facultative psychology of intellect, will, and feeling. If we do not observe this scheme, and let it point our enquiry, we shall fail to understand two crucial elements in Poe: first, that Poe's symbols refer to a known tradition of thought, an intelligible order, apart from what he was as a man, and are not merely the index to a compulsive neurosis; and, secondly, that the symbols, cast into the framework of the three faculties, point towards this larger philosophical dimension, implicit in the serious stories, but very much at the surface in certain of Poe's works that have been almost completely ignored.

I shall discuss here these neglected works: *The Conversation of Eiros and Charmion*, *The Colloquy of Monos and Una*, *The Power of Words*, and *Eureka*. The three first are dialogues between spirits in heaven, after the destruction of the earth; all four set forth a cataclysmic end of the world, modelled on the Christian eschatology. We shall see that *Eureka* goes further, and offers us a semi-rational vision of the final disappearance of the material world into the first spiritual Unity, or God.

It would be folly to try to see in these works the action of a first-rate philosophical mind; there is ingenuity rather than complex thinking. What concerns us is the relation of the semi-philosophical works to Poe's imaginative fiction; that is, a particular relation of the speculative intellect to the work of imagination. I shall have to show that Poe, as a critical mind, had only a distant if impressive insight into the disintegration of the modern personality; and that this insight was not available to him as an imaginative writer, when he had to confront the human situation as a whole man. He was the victim of a disintegration that he seems only intermittently to have understood. Poe is thus a man we must return to: a figure of transition, who retains a traditional insight into a disorder that has since become typical, without being able himself to control it.

Before we examine this insight it will be necessary to fix more clearly in mind than I have yet done the character of Poe as a transitional man. Madame Raïssa Maritain, in a valuable essay, *Magie, Poésie, et Mystique*, says:

> Je ne vois guère de place dans la cosmologie d'Edgar Poe pour des recherches de recettes magiques. Et moins encore dans sa poésie, qui a toujours été parfaitement libre de toute anxiété de ce genre, et dont il n'aurait jamais voulu faire un instrument de pouvoir.

> [I see little place in the cosmology of Edgar Poe for the pursuit of magic recipes. And still less in his poetry, which was always perfectly free of all anxiety of this kind, and of which he never wished to make an instrument of power.]

I am not sure that Madame Maritain is entirely right about the absence of magic, but there is no doubt that Poe *as poet* accepted certain limitations of language. He accepted them in practice. The obscurity of Poe's poetic diction is rather vagueness than the obscurity of complexity; it reflects his uncertain grasp of the relation of language to feeling, and of feeling to nature. But it is never that idolatrous dissolution of language from the grammar of a possible world, which results from the belief that language itself can be reality, or by incantation can create a reality: a superstition that comes down in French from Lautréamont, Rimbaud, and Mallarmé to the Surrealists, and in English to Hart Crane, Wallace Stevens, and Dylan Thomas. (I do not wish it to be understood that I am in any sense "rejecting" these poets, least of all under the rubric "superstition." When men find themselves cut off from reality they will frequently resort to magic rites to recover it—a critical moment of history that has its own relation to reality, from which poetry of great power may emerge.)

Poe, then, accepted his genre *in practice*. If the disorganized, synaesthetic, sensibility arrives in the long run at a corresponding disintegration of the forms of grammar and rhetoric, it must be admitted that Poe stopped short at the mere *doctrine* of synaesthesia. In *The Colloquy of Monos and Una*, the angel Monos describes his passage into the after-life: "The senses were unusually active, although eccentrically so—assuming each other's functions at random. The taste and the smell were inextricably confounded, and became one sentiment, abnormal and intense." But this is not the experience of synaesthesia rendered to our consciousness; to put it as Poe puts it is merely to consider it as a possibility of experience. Eighty years later we find its actuality in the language of an American poet:

> How much I would have bartered! the black gorge
> And all the singular nestings in the hills
> Where beavers learn stitch and tooth.
> The pond I entered once and quickly fled—
> I remember now its singing willow rim.

Rimbaud's "derangement of the senses" is realized. Why did not Poe take the next step and realize it himself? The question is unanswerable, for every writer is who he is, and not somebody else. The discoverer of a new sensibility seldom pushes it as far as language will take it; it largely remains a premonition of something yet to come. Another phase of Poe's disproportion of language and feeling appears in the variations of his prose style, which range from the sobriety and formal elegance of much of his critical writing, to the bathos of stories like *Ligeia* and *Berenice*. When Poe is not involved directly in his own feeling he can be a master of the *ordonnance* of eighteenth century prose; there are passages in *The Narrative of Arthur Gordon Pym* that have the lucidity and intensity of Swift. But when he approaches the full human situation the traditional rhetoric fails him. It becomes in his hands a humorless, insensitive machine whose elaborate motions conceal what it pretends to convey; for without the superimposed order of rhetoric the disorder hidden beneath would explode to the surface,. where he would not be able to manage it. Poe is the transitional figure in modern literature because he discovered our great subject, the disintegration of personality, but kept it in a language that had developed in a tradition of unity and order. Madam Maritain is right in saying that he does not *use* language as magic. But he considers its possibility, and he thinks of language as a potential source of quasi-divine power. He is at the parting of the ways; the two terms of his conflict are thus more prominent than they would appear to be in a writer, or in an age, fully committed to either extreme. "When all are bound for disorder," says Pascal, "none seems to go that way."

Of the three dialogues that I shall discuss here, the first, *The Conversation of Eiros and Charmion*, published in 1839, was the earliest written. It is Poe's first essay at a catastrophic version of the disappearance of the earth: a comet passes over the earth, extracting the nitrogen from the atmosphere and replacing it with oxygen, so that the accelerated oxidation ends in world-wide combustion. But in treating the most umpromising materials Poe means what he says, although the occasions of journalism may not allow him to say all that he means. He *means* the destruction of the world. It is not only a serious possibility, it is a moral and logical necessity of the condition to which man has perversely brought himself.

Man's destruction of his relation to nature is the subject of the next dialogue, *The Colloquy of Monos and Una* (1841). From the perversion of man's nature it follows by a kind of Manichean logic that external nature itself must be destroyed: man's surrender to evil is projected symbolically into the world.

This dialogue, the sequel to *The Conversation of Eiros and Charmion*, is a theological fantasy of the destruction of the earth by fire. I call the vision "theological" because the destruction is not, as it was in the preceding dialogue, merely the result of an interstellar collision. Monos says, "That man, as a race, should not become extinct, I saw that he must be *'born again.'*" Rebirth into the after-life is the mystery that Monos undertakes to explain to Una; but first he makes this long digression:

One word first, my Una, in regard to man's general condition at this epoch. You will remember that one or two of the wise men among our forefathers ... had ventured to doubt the propriety of the term "improvement" as applied to the progress of our civilization. [They uttered] principles which should have taught our race to submit to the guidance of the natural laws, rather than attempt their control. Occasionally the poetic intellect—that intellect which we now feel to have been the most exalted of all—since those truths to us were of the most enduring importance and could only be reached by that *analogy* which speaks in proof-tones to the imagination alone, and to the unaided reason bears no weight—occasionally did this poetic intellect proceed a step farther in the evolving of the vaguely philosophic, and find in the mystic parable that tells of the tree of knowledge ... death-producing, a distinct intimation that knowledge was not meet for man in the infant condition of his soul. ...

Yet these noble exceptions from the general misrule served but to strengthen it by opposition. The great "movement"—that was the cant term—went on: a diseased commotion, moral and physical. Art—the Arts—rose supreme, and, once enthroned, cast chains upon the intellect which had elevated them to power. Even while he stalked a God in his own fancy, an infantine imbecility came over him. As might be supposed from the origin of his disorder, he grew infected with system, and with abstraction. He enwrapped himself in generalities. Among other odd ideas, that of universal equality gained ground; and in the face of analogy and of God—in spite of the laws of graduation so visibly pervading all things ... —wild attempts at an omnipresent Democracy were made. Yet this evil sprang

necessarily from the leading evil—knowledge. . . . Meanwhile huge smoking cities arose, innumerable. Green leaves shrank before the hot breath of furnaces . . . now it appears that we had worked out *our own destruction in the perversion of our taste* [italics mine] or rather in the blind neglect of its culture in the schools. For in truth it was at this crisis that taste alone—that faculty which, *holding a middle position between the pure intellect and the moral sense* [italics mine], could never safely have been disregarded—it was now that taste alone could have led us gently back to Beauty, to Nature, and to Life.

. . . it is not impossible that the sentiment of the natural, had time permitted it, would have regained its old ascendancy over the harsh mathematical reasoning of the schools. . . . This the mass of mankind saw not, or, living lustily although unhappily, affected not to see.

I have quoted the passage at great length in the hope that a certain number of persons at a certain place and time will have read it. Poe's critics (if he has any critics) have not read it. When they refer to it, it is to inform us that Poe was a reactionary Southerner who disliked democracy and industrialism. It would not be wholly to the purpose but it would be edifying to comment on the passage in detail, for it adumbrates a philosophy of impressive extent and depth. When we remember that it was written in the United States in the early 1840's, an era of the American experiment that tolerated very little dissent, we may well wonder whether it was the result of a flash of insight, or of conscious reliance upon a wider European tradition. (My guess is that Poe's idea of "mathematical reasoning" was derived in part from Pascal's *L'esprit de géométrie*, his "taste" from *L'esprit de finesse*. This is a scholarly question that cannot be investigated here.)

A clue to the connection between Poe's historical and metaphysical insight, on the one hand, and the mode of his literary imagination, on the other, may be found in Paul Valéry's essay, "The Position of Baudelaire," where he says:

. . . the basis of Poe's thoughts is associated with a certain personal metaphysical system. But this system, if it directs and dominates and suggests the [literary] theories . . . *by no means penetrates them* [italics mine.].

His metaphysics was not available to him as experience; it did not *penetrate* his imagination. If we will consider together the "harsh mathematical reasoning of the schools" and the theory of the corruption of taste, we shall get a further clue to the Christian philosophical tradition in which Poe consciously or intuitively found himself. Taste is the discipline of feeling according to the laws of the natural order, a discipline of submission to a permanent limitation of man; this discipline has been abrogated by the "mathematical reasoning" whose purpose is the control of nature. Here we have the Cartesian split— taste, feeling, respect for the depth of nature, resolved into a subjectivism which denies the sensible world; for nature has become geometrical, at a high level of abstraction, in which "clear and distinct ideas" only are workable. The sensibility is frustrated, since it is denied its perpetual refreshment in nature: the operative abstraction replaces the rich perspectives of the concrete object. Reason is thus detached from feeling, and likewise from the moral sense, the third and executive member of the psychological triad, moving through the will. Feeling in this scheme being isolated or—as Mr. Scott Buchanan might put it—"occulted," it is strictly speaking without content, and man has lost his access to material forms. We get the hypertrophy of the intellect and the hypertrophy of the will. When neither intellect nor will is bound to the human scale, their projection becomes god-like, and man becomes an angel, in M. Maritain's sense of the term:

> Cartesian dualism breaks man up into two complete substances, joined to one another none knows how: on the one hand, the body which is only geometrical extension; on the other, the soul which is only thought—an angel inhabiting a machine and directing it by means of the pineal gland.
>   . . . for human intellection is living and fresh only when it is centered upon the vigilance of sense perception. The natural roots of our knowledge being cut, a general drying up in philosophy and culture resulted, a drought for which romantic tears were later to provide only an insufficient remedy. . . . Affectivity will have its revenge.

One cannot fail to see here a resemblance, *up to a point*, between the insights of Poe and of Maritain; but at that point appears the profound difference between a catastrophic acceptance and a poised estimation, of the Cartesian dualism. *The Colloquy of Monos and Una* is in the end a romantic tear, and in Poe's tales of perverted nature "affectivity" takes its terrible revenge.

We may discern the precise point at which Poe betrays his surrender to what I shall call the angelic fallacy: it is the point at which his conception of the "poetic intellect" becomes contradictory and obscure. This intellect speaks to us, he says, "by analogy," in "proof tones to the imagination alone." The trap is the adverb *alone*, which contradicts the idea of analogy. He may have meant analogy to the natural world, the higher truths emerging, as they do in Dante, from a rational structure of natural analogy; but he could not have meant all this. And I suppose nobody else in the nineteenth century understood analogy as a mode of knowledge. If the poetic intellect speaks "by analogy" it addresses more than the "imagination alone"; it engages also reason and cognition; for if it alone is addressed there is perhaps a minimum of analogy; if the imagination can work alone, it does so in direct intuition. And in fact in none of the essays and reviews does Poe even consider the idea of analogy. Its single mysterious appearance, in anything like its full historical sense, is in *The Colloquy of Monos and Una*. (It reappears in *Eureka*, where it means simple exemplification or parallelism.) In the "Poetic Principle," the poetic intellect moves independently, with only "incidental" connections with Pure Intellect and the Moral Sense; it is thus committed exclusively to Taste raised to an autonomous faculty. "Imagination is, possibly in man," says Poe in a footnote to his famous review of Halleck and Drake, "a lesser degree of the creative power of God." This is not far from the "esemplastic power" of the Primary Imagination, a Teutonic angel inhabiting a Cartesian machine named Samuel Taylor Coleridge.

Poe's exaltation of the imagination in its Cartesian vacuum fore-shadows a critical dilemma of which we have been acutely aware in our own time. His extravagant claims for poetry do not in any particular exceed, except perhaps in their "period" rhetoric, the claims made by two later generations of English critics represented by Arnold and Richards. "Reli-gion," said Arnold, "is morality touched with emotion." But religion, he said elsewhere, has attached itself to the "fact," by which he meant science; so religion has failed us. Therefore "the future of poetry is immense" because it is its own fact; that is to say, poetry is on its own, whatever its own may be—perhaps its own emotion, which now "touches" poetry instead of reli-gion. Therefore poetry will save us, although it has no connection with the Cartesian machine running outside my window, or inside my vascular system. (Mr. Richards' early views I have discussed on several occasions over many years; I am a little embarrassed to find myself adverting to them again.) In Richards' writings, particularly in a small volume entitled *Science and Poetry* (1926), he tells us that the pseudo-statements of poetry—poetry on its own—cannot stand against the "certified scientific statement" about the facts which for Arnold had already failed both religion and poetry. Neverthe-less poetry will save us because it "orders our minds"—but with what? For Mr. Richards, twenty-five years ago, the Cartesian machine was doing business as usual. Poetry would have to save us by ordering our minds with something that was not true.

Poe's flash of unsustained insight, in *The Colloquy of Monos and Una*, has, I submit, a greater dignity, a deeper philosophical perspective, and a tougher intellectual fibre, than the academic exercises of either Arnold or Mr. Richards. (I still reserve the right to admire both of these men.) Poe is not so isolated as they, in a provincialism of *time*. He still has access, however roundabout, to the great framework of the Aristotelian psychology to which the literature of Europe had been committed for more than two thousand years: this was, and still is for modern critics, an empirical fact that must be confronted if we are to approach literature with anything better than callow systems of psychological analysis, invented overnight, that put the imagina-tive work of the past at a distance seriously greater than that of time.

Poe with perfect tact puts his finger upon the particular function, feeling, that has been blighted by the abstraction of the pure intellect into a transcendental order of its own. He will let neither pure intellect nor the pure moral will (both having been purified of "nature") dominate poetry; he sees that poetry must be centered in the disciplined sense-perception which he inadequately calls taste; and he thus quite rightly opposes the "heresy of the didactic" and the "mathematical reasoning of the schools." He opposes both, but he gives in to the latter. Poe's idolatry of reason, ranging from the cryptogram and the detective story to the panlogism of *Eureka*, is too notorious to need pointing out. The autonomy of the will is in part the theme of the greater stories; and the autonomy of poetry, rising contradictorily and mysteriously from the ruin of its source in feeling, reflects "a lesser degree of the creative power of God." It is the creative power of the Word, man's *spoken* word, an extravagant and slippery pun on the Logos.

I now come to the third dialogue, *The Power of Words*, published in 1845, a fable in which the angelic imagination is pushed beyond the limits of the angelic intelligence to the point at which man considers the possibility of creative power through verbal magic. The angels in this dialogue not only know essence directly; they also have the power of physical creation by means of *words*. We may ask here why, if Poe's insight was as profound as I think it was, he succumbed to a force of disintegration that he understood? An answer to this question is difficult. Insights of the critical intelligence, however impressive, will not always correct, they may never wholly rise above, the subtle and elusive implications of the common language to which the writer is born. As Dante well understood, this is the primary fact of his culture that he has got to reckon with. The culture of the imaginative writer is, first of all, the elementary use of language that he must hear and learn in childhood, and, in the end, not much more than a conscious manipulation of what he had received from life before the age of seven. Poe understood the spiritual disunity that had resulted from the rise of the demi-religion of scientism, but by merely opposing its excesses with equally excessive claims for the "poetic intellect," he subtly perpetuated the disunity from another direction. He set up, if we may be allowed the figure, a parallelogram of forces colliding by chance from unpredicted directions, not proceeding from a central unity. Although he was capable of envisaging the unified action of the mind through the three faculties, his own mind acted upon its materials now as intellect, now as feeling, now as will; never as all three together. Had he not been bred in a society committed to the rationalism of Descartes and Locke by that eminent angel of the rationalistic Enlightenment, Thomas Jefferson? Such commitments probably lie so deep in one's sensibility that mere intellectual conviction, Poe's "unaided reason," can scarcely reach them. Perhaps this discrepancy of belief and feeling exists in all ages, and creates the inner conflicts from which poetry comes. If this points to something in the nature of the literary imagination, we are bound to say that it will always lie a little beyond our understanding.

By the time Poe came to write his fable of the power of words, the angels of omnipotent reason could claim a victory. The scene is again the after-life; the characters two angels who meet in interstellar space after the destruction of the earth—a disaster assumed in all three of the dialogues and in *Eureka*, and a possible eventuality in most of Poe's tales. (One scarcely needs to be reminded of the collapse of the world of Roderick Usher.) The probable meaning of this omnivorous symbol I shall try to glance at presently. The climax of the angels' talk will reveal the long way that Poe had come from the philosophic insight of 1841 to the full angelic vision of 1845:

> *Oinos*—But why, Agathos, do you weep—and why, Oh why do your wings droop as we hover over this fair star—which is the greenest and yet most terrible of all we have encountered in our flight. Its brilliant flowers look like a fairy dream—but its fierce volcanoes like the passions of a turbulent heart.
>
> *Agathos*—They *are*—they *are*! This wild star it is now three centuries since, with clasped hands, and with streaming eyes, at the feet of my beloved—I spoke it—with a few passionate sentences—into birth. Its brilliant flowers *are* the dearest of all unfulfilled dreams, and its raging volcanoes *are* the passions of the most turbulent and unhallowed of hearts.

How had Agathos created this beautiful but unhallowed object? By the "physical power of words," he tells Oinos. Madame Maritain is the only critic I have read who has had the perception to take seriously this dialogue; her comment is of great interest:

> Eh bien, ce texte se réfère-t-il vraiment à une conception magique de la poésie et de la parole? Je ne crois pas. Nous avons affaire ici, comme dans *Eureka*, à une philosophie et une cosmologie panthéistiques, où tout mouvement et toute action participent à l'efficicacité d'une action divine.
>
> [Does the text then really refer to a magical conception of poetry and of the word? I do not think so. We have to do here, as in *Eureka*, with a pantheistic philosophy and cosmology, where every movement and every action participates in the efficiency of a divine action.]

There can be no doubt about Poe's pantheism here and in *Eureka*, but in both works we cannot fail to detect special variations in the direction of deism. Madame Maritain quotes Léon Bloy on the eternal consequences of every action of divine grace for the human spirit, an ancient Christian doctrine connected with the belief in the Community of Saints, for which Pascal invented the great natural analogy:

> The slightest movement affects the whole of nature; a stone cast into the sea changes the whole face of it. So, in the realm of Grace, the smallest act

affects the whole by its results. Therefore everything has its importance.

In every action we must consider, besides the act itself, our present, past, and future conditions, and others whom it touches, and must see the connections of it all. *And so we shall keep ourselves well in check.*

It almost seems as if Poe had just read this passage and had gone at once to his desk to begin *The Power of Words*; as if he had deliberately ignored the moral responsibility, the *check* upon human power, enjoined in the last sentence, and had concentrated upon Pascal's physical analogy for divine grace: "The slightest *movement* affects the whole of nature." One more step, and the "slightest movement," a spoken *word*, will act creatively. A failure of moral responsibility towards the universe would not necessarily issue in an act of physical creation; nor would action undertaken in the state of sanctifying grace produce stars that are both beautiful and hallowed, unless, of course, the *word* is a "magic recipe," incantatory magic, which I believe we undoubtedly get in *The Power of Words*. This is not the same presumption as our own timid, superstitious reverence for an order of poetic language which creates its own reality, but rather a grandiose angelic presumption on the part of man. As usual, Poe is at least partly aware of what he is doing; for Agathos explains:

This power of retrogradation [Pascal's "the smallest action affecting the whole by its results"] in its absolute fulness and perfection—this faculty of referring *all* epochs, *all* effects to *all* causes—is of course the prerogative of the Deity alone—but in every variety of degree, short of absolute perfection, is the power itself exercised by the whole host of the Angelic intelligences.

This "power," of course, is not at this stage magical; it represents angelic knowledge rather than power. But when Agathos created his green star he was not yet an angel; he was still man, but man with the creative power, just short of divine perfection, of the angelic intelligences. Wasn't his power on earth actually greater than that of the angels of Christian theology? For they are not primary creators; they are the powerful but uncreative executives of the divine will. Agathos' doctrine transcends the ideal of mere angelic knowledge: it is superangelism. Man is not only an angel, he is God in his aspect of creativity. I remark almost with regret, mingled with uneasiness, that Poe proves my argument, perhaps too well. (When criticism thinks that it has proved anything, it has become angelic itself.) But this is not all: Oinos tells Agathos that he "remembers many successful experiments in what some philosophers were weak enough to denominate animalculae." And Agathos bows to the mathematicians: "Now the mathematicians . . . saw that the results of any given impulse were absolutely endless . . . these men saw, at the same time, that this species of analysis itself had within itself a capacity for indefinite progress. . . ." Mathematicians were about to achieve the omniscience of the Son, and biologists the creative power of the Father.

Are we to conclude that in these fantasies Poe "appears to yield himself completely to the idea of the moment"? I believe that Mr. Eliot's observation is inaccurate. Poe is quite capable of faking his science, and of appearing to take seriously his own wildest inventions; but the invention is the creaking vehicle of something deeper. What he really takes seriously, and what he yields to in the end, is not an *idea* of the moment. He is progressively mastered by one great idea, deeper than any level of conscious belief and developing to the end of his life at an ever increasing rate, until at last he is engulfed by it. It is his own descent into the maelstrom.

He arrives at it, or reaches the bottom of it, in *Eureka*, which he wrote in 1848, the year before his death. I shall not go so far as to connect, symbolically or prophetically, his death and the vision of the pit at the end of *Eureka*. We may only observe that the complete vision, of which the early works represent an approximation, immediately precedes his death. The proposition of which *Eureka* is to provide the "proof," he states at the beginning:

> In the original unity of the first thing lies the secondary cause of all things, with the germ of their inevitable annihilation.

This "nothingness" is a dialectical conversion, not of one symbol into its opposite by analogy, as we see it in Dante, or even in Donne, but of an abstraction into its antithesis. Thesis: the omniscient intellect of man (of Poe as man) achieves a more than angelic knowledge in comprehending the structure and purpose of the created universe. Antithesis: the final purpose of the created universe is the extinction in its own unity of the omniscient intellect of man. There is no Hegelian synthesis. After the original act of divine creation, God withdraws into his deistic aloofness, leaving the separate and local acts of creation to man. This is the sphere of secondary creations which man as angelic delegate of God is empowered to perform. Thus, says Poe at the end of *Eureka*, not only is every man his own God, every man *is* God: every man the non-spatial center into which the universe, by a reverse motion of the atoms, will contract, as into its annihilation. God destroys himself in the eventual recovery of his unity. Unity equals zero. If Poe must at last "yield himself unto Death utterly," there is a lurid sublimity in the spectacle of his taking God along with him into a grave which is not smaller than the universe.

The material universe is in a state of radical disequilibrium, every atom striving to disengage itself from material forms and to return to the original center; but this is not a center in space. It is the Pascalian center which is the everywhere and nowhere, occupied by nothing. Since matter is merely the dialectical movement of attraction and repulsion, it will have ceased to exist when it rejoins the everywhere and nowhere. Space being emptied of matter, there is not even space, for space is that which is occupied by something. We are beyond the topless and bottomless abyss of Pascal.

The image of the abyss is in all of Poe's serious writings: the mirror in "William Wilson"; burial alive; the "tarn" into which the House of Usher plunges; the great white figure towards which Pym is being borne by a current of the sea; the pit over which the pendulum swings; the dead body containing the living soul of M. Valdemar; being walled up alive; the vertigo of the maelstrom.

Poe's most useful biographer, Professor Quinn, exhibits testimonials from modern physicists to bolster up with scientific authority a work in which he probably has little confidence. Let us assume, what may well be false, that *Eureka* from the scientific point of view of any age is nonsense. That would not make *Eureka* nonsense. "The glory of man," says Valéry in his essay on *Eureka*, "and something more than his glory, is to waste his powers on the void. . . . Thus it would seem that the history of thought can be summarized in these words: *It is absurd by what it seeks; great by what it finds.*" What did Poe's "absurd" essay in eschatology inadvertently find, if indeed it found anything but nothing? Valéry again (and again the French instruct us in Poe) points, in another context, to the central meaning of *Eureka*, without perhaps quite knowing that he has done so (for Paul Valéry was himself an archangel); he says: "As soon as we leave the bounds of the moment, as soon as we attempt to enlarge and extend our presence outside of itself, our forces are exhausted in our liberty." Is this always and under all conditions necessarily true? I think not; but it was particularly true of Poe.

It was true of him because in *Eureka* he circumvented the natural world and tried to put himself not in the presence of God, but in the seat of God. *The exhaustion of force as a consequence of his intellectual liberation from the sensible world*—that is my reading of Valéry as a gloss upon the angelism of Poe. The intellectual force is exhausted because in the end it has no real object. The human intellect cannot reach God as essence; only God as analogy. Analogy to what? Plainly analogy to the natural world; for there is nothing in the intellect that has not previously reached it through the senses. Had Dante arrived at the vision of God by way of sense? We must answer yes, because Dante's Triune Circle is light, which the finite intelligence can see only in what has already been seen by means of it. But Poe's center is that place—to use Dante's great figure—"where the sun is silent." Since he refuses to see nature, he is doomed to see nothing. He has overleaped and cheated the condition of man. The reach of our imaginative enlargement is perhaps no longer than the ladder of analogy, at the top of which we may see all, if we still wish to *see* anything, that we have brought up with us from the bottom, where lies the sensible world. If we take nothing with us to the top but our emptied, angelic intellects, we shall see nothing when we get there. Poe as God sits silent in darkness. Here the movement of tragedy is reversed: there is no action. Man as angel becomes a demon who cannot initiate the first motion of love, and we can feel only compassion with his suffering, for it is potentially ours.

I have not supposed it necessary to describe in detail the structure of *Eureka*, or to call attention to its great passages of expository prose, which seem to me unsurpassed in their kind in the nineteenth century. I have not discussed Poe from what is commonly known as the literary point of view. I have tried to expound one idea, the angelism of the intellect, as one aspect of one writer. I do not hesitate in conclusion to commit Poe's heresy of the didactic, and to point a moral. We shall be so exhausted in our liberty that we shall have to take our final rest, not in the cool of the evening, but in the dark, if any one of our modes decides to set up in business for itself.

RICHARD WILBUR

The House of Poe

A few weeks ago, in the *New York Times Book Review*, Mr. Saul Bellow expressed impatience with the current critical habit of finding symbols in everything. No self-respecting modern professor, Mr. Bellow observed, would dare to explain Achilles' dragging of Hector around the walls of Troy by the mere assertion that Achilles was in a bad temper. That would be too drearily obvious. No, the professor must say that the circular path of Achilles and Hector relates to the theme of circularity which pervades *The Iliad*.

In the following week's *Book Review*, a pedantic correspondent corrected Mr. Bellow, pointing out that Achilles did not, in Homer's *Iliad*, drag Hector's body around the walls of Troy; this perhaps invalidates the Homeric example, but Mr. Bellow's complaint remains, nevertheless, a very sensible one. We are all getting a bit tired, I think, of that laboriously clever criticism which discovers mandalas in Mark Twain, rebirth archetypes in Edwin Arlington Robinson, and fertility myths in everybody.

Still, we must not be carried away by our impatience, to the point of demanding that no more symbols be reported. The business of the critic, after all, is to divine the intention of the work, and to interpret the work in the light of that intention; and since some writers are intentionally symbolic, there is nothing for it but to talk about their symbols. If we speak of Melville, we must speak of symbols. If we speak of Hawthorne, we must speak of symbols. And as for Edgar Allan Poe, whose sesquicentennial year we are met to observe, I think we can make no sense about him until we consider his work—and in particular his prose fiction—as deliberate and often brilliant allegory.

Not everyone will agree with me that Poe's work has an accessible

From *Anniversary Lectures 1959*. Copyright © 1966 by Richard Wilbur.

allegorical meaning. Some critics, in fact, have refused to see any substance, allegorical or otherwise, in Poe's fiction, and have regarded his tales as nothing more than complicated machines for saying "boo." Others have intuited undiscoverable meanings in Poe, generally of an unpleasant kind: I recall one Freudian critic declaring that if we find Poe unintelligible we should congratulate ouselves, since if we *could* understand him it would be proof of our abnormality.

It is not really surprising that some critics should think Poe meaning-less, or that others should suppose his meaning intelligible only to monsters. Poe was not a wide-open and perspicuous writer; indeed, he was a secretive writer both by temperament and by conviction. He sprinkled his stories with sly references to himself and to his personal history. He gave his own birthday of January 19 to his character William Wilson; he bestowed his own height and color of eye on the captain of the phantom ship in "Ms. Found in a Bottle"; and the name of one of his heroes, Arthur Gordon Pym, is patently a version of his own. He was a maker and solver of puzzles, fascinated by codes, ciphers, anagrams, acrostics, hieroglyphics, and the Kabbala. He invented the detective story. He was fond of aliases; he delighted in accounts of swindles; he perpetrated the famous Balloon Hoax of 1844; and one of his most characteristic stories is entitled "Mystification." A man so devoted to concealment and deception and unraveling and detection might be expected to have in his work what Poe himself called "undercurrents of meaning."

And that is where Poe, as a critic, said that meaning belongs: not on the surface of the poem or tale, but below the surface as a dark undercurrent. If the meaning of a work is made overly clear—as Poe said in his "Philosophy of Composition"—if the meaning is brought to the surface and made the upper current of the poem or tale, then the work becomes bald and prosaic and ceases to be art. Poe conceived of art, you see, not as a means of giving imaginative order to earthly experience, but as a stimulus to unearthly visions. The work of literary art does not, in Poe's view, present the reader with a provisional arrangement of reality; instead, it seeks to disengage the reader's mind from reality and propel it toward the ideal. Now, since Poe thought the function of art was to set the mind soaring upward in what he called "a wild effort to reach the Beauty above," it was important to him that the poem or tale should not have such definiteness and completeness of meaning as might contain the reader's mind within the work. Therefore Poe's criticism places a positive value on the obscuration of meaning, on a dark suggestiveness, on a deliberate vagueness by means of which the reader's mind may be set adrift toward the beyond.

Poe's criticism, then, assures us that his work does have meaning. And Poe also assures us that this meaning is not on the surface but in the depths. If we accept Poe's invitation to play detective, and commence to read him with an eye for submerged meaning, it is not long before we sense that there *are* meanings to be found, and that in fact many of Poe's stories, though superficially dissimilar, tell the same tale. We begin to have this sense as we notice Poe's repeated use of certain narrative patterns; his repetition of certain words and phrases; his use, in story after story, of certain scenes and properties. We notice, for instance, the recurrence of the *spiral* or *vortex*. In "Ms. Found in a Bottle," the story ends with a plunge into a whirlpool; the "Descent into the Maelström" also concludes in a watery vortex; the house of Usher, just before it plunges into the tarn, is swaddled in a whirlwind; the hero of "Metzengerstein," Poe's first published story, perishes in "a whirlwind of chaotic fire"; and at the close of "King Pest," Hugh Tarpaulin is cast into a puncheon of ale and disappears "amid a whirlpool of foam." That Poe offers us so many spirals or vortices in his fiction, and that they should always appear at the same terminal point in their respective narratives, is a strong indication that the spiral had some symbolic value for Poe. And it did: What the spiral invariably represents in any tale of Poe's is the loss of consciousness, and the descent of the mind into sleep.

I hope you will grant, before I am through, that to find spirals in Poe is not so silly as finding circles in Homer. The professor who finds circles in Homer does so to the neglect of more important and more provable meanings. But the spiral or vortex is a part of that symbolic language in which Poe said his say, and unless we understand it we cannot understand Poe.

But now I have gotten ahead of myself, and before I proceed with my project of exploring one area of Poe's symbolism, I think I had better say something about Poe's conception of poetry and the poet.

Poe conceived of God as a poet. The universe, therefore, was an artistic creation, a poem composed by God. Now, if the universe is a poem, it follows that the one proper response to it is aesthetic, and that God's creatures are attuned to Him in proportion as their imaginations are ravished by the beauty and harmony of his creation. Not to worship beauty, not to regard poetic knowledge as divine, would be to turn one's back on God and fall from grace.

The planet Earth, according to Poe's myth of the cosmos, has done just this. It has fallen away from God by exalting the scientific reason above poetic intuition, and by putting its trust in material fact rather than in visionary knowledge. The Earth's inhabitants are thus corrupted by rationalism and materialism; their souls are diseased; and Poe sees this disease of the human spirit as having contaminated physical nature. The woods and fields and waters of Earth have thereby lost their first beauty, and no longer clearly express God's imagination; the landscape has lost its original perfection of composition, in proportion as men have lost their power to perceive the beautiful.

Since Earth is a fallen planet, life upon Earth is necessarily a torment for the poet: neither in the human sphere nor in the realm of nature can he find fit objects for contemplation, and indeed his soul is oppressed by everything around him. The rationalist mocks at him; the dull, prosaic spirit of the age damps his imaginative spark; the gross materiality of the world crowds in upon him. His only recourse is to abandon all concern for Earthly things, and to devote himself as purely as possible to unearthly visions, in hopes of glimpsing that heavenly beauty which is the thought of God.

Poe, then, sees the poetic soul as at war with the mundane physical world; and that warfare is Poe's fundamental subject. But the war between soul and world is not the only war. There is also warfare within the poet's very nature. To be sure, the poet's nature was not always in conflict with itself. Prior to his earthly incarnation, and during his dreamy chidhood, Poe's poet enjoyed a serene unity of being; his consciousness was purely imaginative, and he knew the universe for the divine poem that it is. But with his entrance into adult life, the poet became involved with a fallen world in which the physical, the factual, the rational, the prosaic are not escapable. Thus, compromised, he lost his perfect spirituality, and is now cursed with a divided nature. Though his imagination still yearns toward ideal beauty, his mortal body chains him to the physical and temporal and local; the hungers and passions of his body draw him toward external objects, and the conflict of conscience and desire degrades and distracts his soul; his mortal senses try to convince him of the reality of a material world which his soul struggles to escape; his reason urges him to acknowledge everyday fact, and to confine his thought within the prison of logic. For all these reasons it is not easy for the poet to detach his soul from earthly things, and regain his lost imaginative power—his power to commune with that supernal beauty which is symbolized, in Poe, by the shadowy and angelic figures of Ligeia, and Helen, and Lenore.

These, then, are Poe's great subjects: first, the war between the poetic soul and the external world; second, the war between the poetic soul and the earthly self to which it is bound. All of Poe's major stories are allegorical presentations of these conflicts, and everything he wrote bore somehow upon them.

How does one wage war against the external world? And how does one release one's visionary soul from the body, and from the constraint of the reason? These may sound like difficult tasks; and yet we all accomplish them every night. In a subjective sense—and Poe's thought is wholly subjective—we destroy the world every time we close our eyes. If *esse est percipi*, as Bishop Berkeley said—if to be is to be perceived—then when we withdraw our attention from the world in somnolence or sleep, the world ceases to be. As our minds move toward sleep, by way of drowsiness and reverie and the hypnagogic state, we escape from consciousness of the world, we escape from awareness of our bodies, and we enter a realm in which reason no longer hampers the play of the imagination: we enter the realm of dream.

Like many romantic poets, Poe identified imagination with dream. Where Poe differed from other romantic poets was in the literalness and absoluteness of the identification, and in the clinical precision with which he observed the phenomena of dream, carefully distinguishing the various states through which the mind passes on its way to sleep. A large number of Poe's stories derive their very structure from this sequence of mental states: "Ms. Found in a Bottle," to give but one example, is an allegory of the mind's voyage from the waking world into the world of dreams, with each main step of the narrative symbolizing the passage of the mind from one state to another—from wakefulness to reverie, from reverie to the hypnagogic state, from the hypnagogic state to the deep dream. The departure of the narrator's ship from Batavia represents the mind's withdrawal from the waking world; the drowning of the captain and all but one of the crew represents the growing solitude of reverie; when the narrator is transferred by collision from a real ship to a phantom ship, we are to understand that he has passed from reverie, a state in which reality and dream exist in a kind of equilibrium, into the free fantasy of the hypnagogic state. And when the phantom ship makes its final plunge into the whirlpool, we are to understand that the narrator's mind has gone over the brink of sleep and descended into dreams.

What I am saying by means of this example is that the scenes and situations of Poe's tales are always concrete representations of states of mind. If we bear in mind Poe's fundamental plot—the effort of the poetic soul to escape all consciousness of the world in dream—we soon recognize the significance of certain scenic or situational motifs which turn up in story after story. The most important of these recurrent motifs is that of *enclosure* or *circumscription*; perhaps the latter term is preferable, because it is Poe's own word, and because Poe's enclosures are so often more or less circular in form. The heroes of Poe's tales and poems are violently circumscribed by whirl-pools, or peacefully circumscribed by cloud-capped Paradisal valleys; they float upon circular pools ringed in by steep flowering hillsides; they dwell on islands, or voyage to them; we find Poe's heroes also in coffins, in the cabs of balloons, or hidden away in the holds of ships; and above all we find them sitting alone in the claustral and richly furnished rooms of remote and mouldering mansions.

Almost never, if you think about it, is one of Poe's heroes to be seen standing in the light of common day; almost never does the Poe hero breathe the air that others breathe; he requires some kind of envelope in order to be what he is; he is always either enclosed or on his way to an enclosure. The narrative of William Wilson conducts the hero from Stoke Newington to Eton, from Eton to Oxford, and then to Rome by way of Paris, Vienna, Berlin, Moscow, Naples, and Egypt: and yet, for all his travels, Wilson seems never to set foot out-of-doors. The story takes place in a series of rooms, the last one locked from the inside.

Sometimes Poe emphasizes the circumscription of his heroes by multiple enclosures. Roderick Usher dwells in a great and crumbling mansion from which, as Poe tells us, he has not ventured forth in many years. This mansion stands islanded in a stagnant lake, which serves it as a defensive moat. And beyond the moat lies the Usher estate, a vast barren tract having its own peculiar and forbidding weather and atmosphere. You might say that Roderick Usher is defended in depth; and yet at the close of the story Poe compounds Roderick's inaccessibility by having the mansion and its occupant swallowed up by the waters of the tarn.

What does it mean that Poe's heroes are invariably enclosed or circumscribed? The answer is simple: circumscription, in Poe's tales, means the exclusion from consciousness of the so-called real world, the world of time and reason and physical fact; it means the isolation of the poetic soul in visionary reverie or trance. When we find one of Poe's characters in a remote valley, or a claustral room, we know that he is in the process of dreaming his way out of the world.

Now, I want to devote the time remaining to the consideration of one kind of enclosure in Poe's tales: the mouldering mansion and its richly furnished rooms. I want to concentrate on Poe's architecture and décor for two reasons: first, because Poe's use of architecture is so frankly and provably allegorical that I *should* be able to be convincing about it; second, because by concentrating on one area of Poe's symbolism we shall be able to see that his stories are allegorical not only in their broad patterns, but also in their smallest details.

Let us begin with a familiar poem, "The Haunted Palace." The opening stanzas of this poem, as a number of critics have noted, make a point-by-point comparison between a building and the head of a man. The exterior of the palace represents the man's physical features; the interior represents the man's mind engaged in harmonious imaginative thought.

> In the greenest of our valleys
>   By good angels tenanted,
> Once a fair and stately palace—
>   Radiant palace—reared its head.
> In the monarch Thought's dominion—
>   It stood there!
> Never seraph spread a pinion
>   Over fabric half so fair!

Banners yellow, glorious, golden,
　　On its roof did float and flow,
(This—all this—was in the olden
　　Time long ago,)
And every gentle air that dallied,
　　In that sweet day,
Along the ramparts plumed and pallid,
　　A wingéd odor went away.

Wanderers in that happy valley,
　　Through two luminous windows, saw
Spirits moving musically,
　　To a lute's well-tunéd law,
Round about a throne where, sitting,
　　Porphyrogene,
In state his glory well befitting,
　　The ruler of the realm was seen.

And all in pearl and ruby glowing
　　Was the fair palace door,
Through which came flowing, flowing, flowing,
　　And sparkling evermore,
A troop of Echoes, whose sweet duty
　　Was but to sing,
In voices of surpassing beauty,
　　The wit and wisdom of their king.

I expect you observed that the two luminous windows of the palace are the eyes of a man, and that the yellow banners on the roof are his luxuriant blond hair. The "pearl and ruby" door is the man's mouth—ruby representing red lips, and pearl representing pearly white teeth. The beautiful Echoes which issue from the pearl and ruby door are the poetic utterances of the man's harmonious imagination, here symbolized as an orderly dance. The angel-guarded valley in which the palace stands, and which Poe describes as "the monarch Thought's dominion," is a symbol of the man's exclusive awareness of exalted and spiritual things. The valley is what Poe elsewhere called "that evergreen and radiant paradise which the true poet knows . . . as the limited realm of his authority, as the circumscribed Eden of his dreams."

As you all remember, the last two stanzas of the poem describe the physical and spiritual corruption of the palace and its domain, and it was to this part of the poem that Poe was referring when he told a correspondent, "By the 'Haunted Palace' I mean to imply a mind haunted by phantoms—a disordered brain." Let me read you the closing lines:

But evil things, in robes of sorrow,
　　Assailed the monarch's high estate.
(Ah, let us mourn!—for never morrow
　　Shall dawn upon him desolate!)

> And round about his home the glory
>   That blushed and bloomed,
> Is but a dim-remembered story
>   Of the old time entombed.
>
> And travellers, now, within that valley,
>   Through the red-litten windows see
> Vast forms, that move fantastically
>   To a discordant melody,
> While, like a ghastly rapid river,
>   Through the pale door
> A hideous throng rush out forever
>   And laugh—but smile no more.

The domain of the monarch Thought, in these final stanzas, is disrupted by civil war, and in consequence everything alters for the worse. The valley becomes barren, like the domain of Roderick Usher; the eye-like windows of the palace are no longer "luminous," but have become "red-litten"—they are like the bloodshot eyes of a madman or a drunkard. As for the mouth of our allegorized man, it is now "pale" rather than "pearl and ruby," and through it come no sweet Echoes, as before, but the wild laughter of a jangling and discordant mind.

The two states of the palace—before and after—are, as we can see, two states of mind. Poe does not make it altogether clear *why* one state of mind has given way to the other, but by recourse to similar tales and poems we can readily find the answer. The palace in its original condition expresses the imaginative harmony which the poet's soul enjoys in early childhood, when all things are viewed with a tyrannical and unchallenged subjectivity. But as the soul passes from childhood into adult life, its consciousness is more and more invaded by the corrupt and corrupting external world: it succumbs to passion, it develops a conscience, it makes concessions to reason and to objective fact. Consequently, there is civil war in the palace of the mind. The imagination must now struggle against the intellect and the moral sense; finding itself no longer able to possess the world through a serene solipsism, it strives to annihilate the outer world by turning in upon itself; it flees into irrationality and dream; and all its dreams are efforts both to recall and to simulate its primal, unfallen state. "The Haunted Palace" presents us with a possible key to the general meaning of Poe's architecture; and this key proves, if one tries it, to open every building in Poe's fiction. Roderick Usher, as you will remember, declaims "The Haunted Palace" to the visitor who tells his story, accompanying the poem with wild improvisations on the guitar. We are encouraged, therefore, to compare the palace of the poem with the house of the story; and it is no surprise to find that the Usher mansion has "vacant eye-like windows," and that there are mysterious physical sympathies between Roderick Usher and the house in which he dwells. The House of Usher *is*, in allegorical fact, the physical body of Roderick Usher, and its dim interior *is*, in fact, Roderick Usher's visionary mind.

The House of Usher, like many edifices in Poe, is in a state of extreme decay. The stonework of its facade has so crumbled and decomposed that it reminds the narrator, as he puts it, "of the specious totality of old wood-work which has rotted for long years in some neglected vault." The Usher mansion is so eaten away, so fragile, that it seems a breeze would push it over; it remains standing only because the atmosphere of Usher's domain is perfectly motionless and dead. Such is the case also with the "time-eaten towers that tremble not" in Poe's poem "The City in the Sea"; and likewise the magnificent architecture of "The Domain of Arnheim" is said to "sustain itself by a miracle in mid-air." Even the detective Dupin lives in a perilously decayed structure: the narrator of "The Murders in the Rue Morgue" tells how he and Dupin dwelt in a "time-eaten and grotesque mansion, long deserted through superstitions into which we did not enquire, and tottering to its fall in a retired and desolate portion of the Faubourg St. Germain." (Notice how, even when Poe's buildings are situated in cities, he manages to circumscribe them with a protective desolation.)

We must now ask what Poe means by the extreme and tottering decay of so many of his structures. The answer is best given by reference to "The Fall of the House of Usher," and in giving the answer we shall arrive, I think, at an understanding of the pattern of that story.

"The Fall of the House of Usher" is a journey into the depths of the self. I have said that all journeys in Poe are allegories of the process of dreaming, and we must understand "The Fall of the House of Usher" as a dream of the narrator's, in which he leaves behind him the waking, physical world and journeys inward toward his *moi intérieur*, toward his inner and spiritual self. That inner and spiritual self is Roderick Usher.

Roderick Usher, then, is a part of the narrator's self, which the narrator reaches by way of reverie. We may think of Usher, if we like, as the narrator's imagination, or as his visionary soul. Or we may think of him as a *state of mind* which the narrator enters at a certain stage of his progress into dreams. Considered as a state of mind, Roderick Usher is an allegorical figure representing the hypnagogic state.

The hypnagogic state, about which there is strangely little said in the literature of psychology, is a condition of semi-consciousness in which the closed eye beholds a continuous procession of vivid and constantly changing forms. These forms sometimes have color, and are often abstract in character. Poe regarded the hypnagogic state as the visionary condition *par excellence*, and he considered its rapidly shifting abstract images to be—as he put it—"glimpses of the spirit's outer world." These visionary glimpses, Poe says in one of his Marginalia, "arise in the soul . . . only . . . at those mere points of time where the confines of the waking world blend with those of the world of dreams." And Poe goes on to say: "I am aware of these 'fancies' only when I am upon the very brink of sleep, with the consciousness that I am so."

Roderick Usher enacts the hypnagogic state in a number of ways. For one thing, the narrator describes Roderick's behavior as inconsistent, and characterized by constant alternation: he is alternately vivacious and sullen; he is alternately communicative and rapt; he speaks at one moment with "tremulous indecision," and at the next with the "energetic concision" of an excited opium-eater. His conduct resembles, in other words, that wavering between consciousness and subconsciousness which characterizes the hypnagogic state. The trembling of Roderick's body, and the floating of his silken hair, also bring to mind the instability and underwater quality of hypnagogic images. His improvisations on the guitar suggest hypnagogic experience in their rapidity, changeableness, and wild novelty. And as for Usher's paintings, which the narrator describes as "pure abstractions," they quite simply *are* hypnagogic images. The narrator says of Roderick, "From the paintings over which his elaborate fancy brooded, and which grew, touch by touch, into vaguenesses at which I shuddered the more thrillingly because I shuddered without knowing why—from these paintings (vivid as their images now are before me) I would in vain endeavor to educe more than a small portion which should lie within the compass of merely written words." That the narrator finds Roderick's paintings indescribable is interesting, because in that one of the Marginalia from which I have quoted, Poe asserts that the only things in human experience which lie "beyond the compass of words" are the visions of the hypnagogic state.

Roderick Usher stands for the hypnagogic state, which as Poe said is a teetering condition of mind occurring "upon the very brink of sleep." Since Roderick is the embodiment of a state of mind in which *falling*—falling asleep—is imminent, it is appropriate that the building which symbolizes his mind should promise at every moment to fall. The House of Usher stares down broodingly at its reflection in the tarn below, as in the hypnagogic state the conscious mind may stare into the subconscious; the house threatens continually to collapse because it is extremely easy for the mind to slip from the hypnagogic state into the depths of sleep; and when the House of Usher *does* fall, the story ends, as it must, because the mind, at the end of its inward journey, has plunged into the darkness of sleep.

We have found one allegorical meaning in the tottering decay of Poe's buildings; there is another meaning, equally important, which may be stated very briefly. I have said that Poe saw the poet as at war with the material world, and with the material or physical aspects of himself; and I have said that Poe identified poetic imagination with the power to escape from the material and the materialistic, to exclude them from consciousness and so subjectively destroy them. Now, if we recall these things, and recall also that the exteriors of Poe's houses or palaces, with their eye-like windows and mouth-like doors, represent the physical features of Poe's dreaming heroes, then the characteristic dilapidation of Poe's architecture takes on sudden significance. The extreme decay of the House of Usher—a decay so extreme as to approach the atmospheric—is quite simply a sign that the narrator, in reaching that state of mind which he calls Roderick Usher, has very nearly dreamt himself free of his physical body, and of the material world with which that body connects him.

This is what decay or decomposition mean everywhere in Poe; and we find them almost everywhere. Poe's preoccupation with decay is not, as some critics have thought, an indication of necrophilia; decay in Poe is a symbol of visionary remoteness from the physical, a sign that the state of mind represented is one of almost pure spirituality. When the House of Usher disintegrates or dematerializes at the close of the story, it does so because Roderick Usher has become all soul. "The Fall of the House of Usher," then, is not really a horror story; it is a triumphant report by the narrator that it *is* possible for the poetic soul to shake off this temporal, rational, physical world and escape, if only for a moment, to a realm of unfettered vision.

We have now arrived at three notions about Poe's typical building. It is set apart in a valley or a sea or a waste place, and this remoteness is intended to express the retreat of the poet's mind from worldly consciousness into dream. It is a tottery structure, and this indicates that the dreamer within is in that unstable threshold condition called the hypnagogic state. Finally, Poe's typical building is crumbling or decomposing, and this means that the dreamer's mind is moving toward a perfect freedom from his material self and the material world. Let us now open the door—or mouth—of Poe's building and visit the mind inside.

As we enter the palace of the visionary hero of "The Assignation," or the house of Roderick Usher, we find ourselves approaching the master's private chamber by way of dim and winding passages, or a winding staircase. There is no end to dim windings in Poe's fiction: there are dim and winding woods paths, dim and winding streets, dim and winding watercourses—and, whenever the symbolism is architectural, there are likely to be dim and winding passages or staircases. It is not at all hard to guess what Poe means by this symbol. If we think of waking life as dominated by reason, and if we think of the reason as a daylight faculty which operates in straight lines, then it is proper that reverie should be represented as an obscure and wandering movement of the mind. There are other, and equally obvious meanings in Poe's symbol of dim and winding passages: to grope through such passages is to become confused as to place and direction, just as in reverie we begin to lose any sense of locality, and to have an infinite freedom in regard to space. In his description of the huge old mansion in which William Wilson went to school, Poe makes this meaning of winding passages very plain:

> But the house!—how quaint an old building was this!—to me how veritable a palace of enchantment! There was no end to its windings—to its incomprehensible subdivisions. It was difficult, at any given time, to say with certainty upon which of its two stories one happened to be. From each room to every other there were sure to be found three or four steps either in ascent or descent. Then the lateral branches were innumerable—inconceivable—and so returning in upon themselves, that our most exact ideas in regard to the whole mansion were not very far different from those with which we pondered on infinity.

Dim windings indicate the state of reverie; they point toward that infinite freedom in and from space which the mind achieves in dreams; also, in their curvature and in their occasional doubling-back, they anticipate the mind's final spiralling plunge into unconsciousness. But the immediate goal of reverie's winding passages is that magnificent chamber in which we find the visionary hero slumped in a chair or lolling on an ottoman, occupied in purging his consciousness of everything that is earthly.

Since I have been speaking of geometry—of straight lines and curves and spirals—perhaps the first thing to notice about Poe's dream rooms is their shape. It has already been said that the enclosures of Poe's tales incline to a curving or circular form. And Poe himself, in certain of his essays and dialogues, explains this inclination by denouncing what he calls "the harsh mathematical reason of the schools," and complaining that practical science has covered the face of the earth with "rectangular obscenities." Poe quite explicitly identifies regular angular forms with everyday reason, and the circle, oval, or fluid arabesque with the otherworldly imagination. Therefore, if we discover that the dream chambers of Poe's fiction are free of angular regularity, we may be sure that we are noticing a pointed and purposeful consistency in his architecture and décor.

The ball-room of the story "Hop-Frog" is circular. The Devil's apartment in "The Duc de l'Omelette" has its corners "rounded into niches," and we find rounded corners also in Poe's essay "The Philosophy of Furniture." In "Ligeia," the bridal chamber is a pentagonal turret room; however, the angles are concealed by sarcophagi, so that the effect is circular. The corners of Roderick Usher's chamber are likewise concealed, being lost in deep shadow.

Other dream rooms are either irregular or indeterminate in form. For example, there are the seven rooms of Prince Prospero's imperial suite in "The Masque of the Red Death." As Poe observes, "in many palaces . . . such suites form a long and straight vista"; but in Prince Prospero's palace, as he describes it, "the apartments were so irregularly disposed that the vision embraced but little more than one at a time. There was a sharp turn at every twenty or thirty yards, and at each turn a novel effect." The turret room of *The Oval Portrait* is not defined as to shape; we are told, however, that it is architecturally "bizarre," and complicated by a quantity of unexpected nooks and niches. Similarly, the visionary's apartment in "The Assignation" is described only as dazzling, astounding and original in its architecture; we are not told in what way its dimensions are peculiar, but it seems safe to assume that it would be a difficult room to measure for wall-to-wall carpeting. The room of "The Assignation," by the way—like that of "Ligeia"—has its walls enshrouded in rich figured draperies which are continually agitated by some mysterious agency. The fluid shifting of the figures suggests, of course, the behavior of hypnagogic images; but the agitation of the draperies would also produce a perpetual ambiguity of architectural form, and the effect would resemble that which Pevsner ascribes to the interior of San Vitale in Ravenna: "a sensation of uncertainty [and] of a dreamlike floating."

Poe, as you see, is at great pains to avoid depicting the usual squarish sort of room in which we spend much of our waking lives. His chambers of dream either approximate the circle—an infinite form which is, as Poe somewhere observes, "the emblem of Eternity"—or they so lack any apprehensible regularity of shape as to suggest the changeableness and spatial freedom of the dreaming mind. The exceptions to this rule are few and entirely explainable. I will grant, for instance, that the iron-walled torture chamber of "The Pit and the Pendulum" portrays the very reverse of spatial freedom, and that it is painfully angular in character, the angles growing more acute as the torture intensifies. But there is a very good allegorical reason for these things. The rooms of "Ligeia" or "The Assignation" symbolize a triumphantly imaginative state of mind in which the dreamer is all but free of the so-called "real" world. In "The Pit and the Pendulum," the dream is of quite another kind; it is a nightmare state, in which the dreamer is imaginatively impotent, and can find no refuge from reality, even in dream. Though he lies on the brink of the pit, on the very verge of the plunge into unconsciousness, he is still unable to disengage himself from the physical and temporal world. The physical oppresses him in the shape of lurid graveyard visions; the temporal oppresses him in the form of an enormous and deadly pendulum. It is altogether appropriate, then, that this particular chamber should be constricting and cruelly angular.

But let us return to Poe's typical room, and look now at its furnishings.

They are generally weird, magnificent, and suggestive of great wealth. The narrator of "The Assignation," entering the hero's apartment, feels "blind and dizzy with luxuriousness," and looking about him he confesses, "I could not bring myself to believe that the wealth of any subject in Europe could have supplied the princely magnificence which burned and blazed around." Poe's visionaries are, as a general thing, extremely rich; the hero of "Ligeia" confides that, as for wealth, he possesses "far more, very far more, than ordinarily falls to the lot of mortals"; and Ellison, in "The Domain of Arnheim," is the fortunate inheritor of 450 million dollars. Legrand, in "The Gold Bug," with his treasure of 450 *thousand*, is only a poor relation of Mr. Ellison; still, by ordinary standards, he seems sublimely solvent.

Now, we must be careful to take all these riches in an allegorical sense. As we contemplate the splendor of any of Poe's rooms, we must remember that the room is a state of mind, and that everything in it is therefore a thought, a mental image. The allegorical meaning of the costliness of Poe's décor is simply this: that his heroes are richly imaginative. And since imagination is a gift rather than an acquisition, it is appropriate that riches in Poe should be inherited or found, but never earned.

Another thing we notice about Poe's furnishings is that they are eclectic in the extreme. Their richness is not the richness of Tiffany's and Sloan's, but of all periods and all cultures. Here is a partial inventory of the fantastic bridal-chamber in "Ligeia": Egyptian carvings and sarcophagi; Venetian glass; fretwork of a semi-Gothic, semi-Druidical character; a Saracenic chandelier; Oriental ottomans and candelabra; an Indian couch; and figured draperies with Norman motifs. The same defiance of what interior decorators once called "keeping" is found in the apartment of the visionary hero of "The Assignation," and one of that hero's speeches hints at the allegorical meaning of his jumbled décor:

> To dream [says the hero of "The Assignation"]—to dream has been the business of my life. I have therefore framed for myself, as you see, a bower of dreams. In the heart of Venice could I have erected a better? You behold around you, it is true, a medley of architectural embellishments. The chastity of Ionia is offended by antediluvian devices, and the sphynxes of Egypt are outstretched upon carpets of gold. Yet the effect is incongruous to the timid alone. Proprieties of place, and especially of time, are the bugbears which terrify mankind from the contemplation of the magnificent.

That last sentence, with its scornful reference to "proprieties of place, and . . . time," should put us in mind of the first stanza of Poe's poem "Dream-Land":

> By a route obscure and lonely,
> Haunted by ill angels only,

Where an Eidolon, named NIGHT,
On a black throne reigns upright,
I have reached these lands but newly
From an ultimate dim Thule—
From a wild weird clime that lieth, sublime,
Out of SPACE—out of TIME.

In dream-land, we are "out of SPACE—out of TIME," and the same is true of such apartments or "bowers of dreams" as the hero of "The Assignation" inhabits. His eclectic furnishings, with their wild juxtapositions of Venetian and Indian, Egyptian and Norman, are symbolic of the visionary soul's transcendence of spatial and temporal limitations. When one of Poe's dream-rooms is *not* furnished in the fashion I have been describing, the idea of spatial and temporal freedom is often conveyed in some other manner: Roderick Usher's library, for instance, with its rare and precious volumes belonging to all times and tongues, is another concrete symbol of the timelessness and placelessness of the dreaming mind.

We have spoken of the winding approaches to Poe's dream chambers, of their curvilinear or indeterminate shape, and of the rich eclecticism of their furnishings. Let us now glance over such matters as lighting, sound-proofing, and ventilation. As regards lighting, the rooms of Poe's tales are never exposed to the naked rays of the sun, because the sun belongs to the waking world and waking consciousness. The narrator of "The Murders in the Rue Morgue" tells how he and his friend Dupin conducted their lives in such a way as to avoid all exposure to sunlight. "At the first dawn of the morning," he writes, "we closed all the massy shutters of our old building; lighting a couple of tapers which, strongly perfumed, threw out only the ghastliest and feeblest of rays. By the aid of these we then busied our souls in dreams . . ."

In some of Poe's rooms, there simply are no windows. In other cases, the windows are blocked up or shuttered. When the windows are not blocked or shuttered, their panes are tinted with a crimson or leaden hue, so as to transform the light of day into a lurid or ghastly glow. This kind of lighting, in which the sun's rays are admitted but transformed, belongs to the portrayal of those half-states of mind in which dream and reality are blended. Filtered through tinted panes, the sunlight enters certain of Poe's rooms as it might enter the half-closed eyes of a daydreamer, or the dream-dimmed eyes of someone awakening from sleep. But when Poe wishes to represent that deeper phase of dreaming in which visionary consciousness has all but annihilated any sense of the external world, the lighting is always artificial and the time is always night.

Flickering candles, wavering torches, and censers full of writhing varicolored flames furnish much of the illumination of Poe's rooms, and one can see the appropriateness of such lighting to the vague and shifting percep-tions of the hypnagogic state. But undoubtedly the most important lighting-fixture in Poe's rooms—and one which appears in a good half of them—is the chandelier. It hangs from the lofty ceiling by a long chain, generally of gold, and it consists sometimes of a censer, sometimes of a lamp, sometimes of candles, sometimes of a glowing jewel (a ruby or a diamond), and once, in the macabre tale "King Pest," of a skull containing ignited charcoal. What we must understand about this chandelier, as Poe explains in his poem "Al Aaraaf," is that its chain does not stop at the ceiling: it goes right on through the ceiling, through the roof, and up to heaven. What comes down the chain from heaven is the divine power of imagination, and it is imagination's purifying fire which flashes or flickers from the chandelier. That is why the immaterial and angelic Ligeia makes her reappearance directly beneath the chandelier; and that is why Hop-Frog makes his departure for dream-land by climbing the chandelier chain and vanishing through the skylight.

The dreaming soul, then, has its own light—a light more spiritual, more divine, than that of the sun. And Poe's chamber of dream is autono-mous in every other respect. No breath of air enters it from the outside world: either its atmosphere is dead, or its draperies are stirred by magical and intramural air currents. No earthly sound invades the chamber: either it is deadly still, or it echoes with a sourceless and unearthly music. Nor does any odor of flower or field intrude: instead, as Poe tells in "The Assignation," the sense of smell is "oppressed by mingled and conflicting perfumes, reeking up from strange convolute censers."

The point of all this is that the dreaming psyche separates itself wholly from the bodily senses—the "rudimental senses," as Poe called them. The bodily senses are dependent on objective stimuli—on the lights and sounds and odors of the physical world. But the sensuous life of dream is self-sufficient and immaterial, and consists in the imagination's Godlike enjoyment of its own creations.

I am reminded, at this point, of a paragraph of Santayana's, in which he describes the human soul as it was conceived by the philosopher Leibniz. Leibniz, says Santayana, assigned

> a mental seat to all sensible objects. The soul, he said, had no windows and, he might have added, no doors; no light could come to it from without; and it could not exert any transitive force or make any difference beyond its own insulated chamber. It was a *camera obscura*, with a universe painted on its impenetrable walls. The changes which went on in it were like those in a dream, due to the discharge of pent-up energies and fecundities within it . . .

Leibniz' chamber of the soul is identical with Poe's chamber of dream: but the solipsism which Leibniz saw as the normal human condition was for

Poe an ideal state, a blessed state, which we may enjoy as children or as pre-existent souls, but can reclaim in adult life only by a flight from everyday consciousness into hypnagogic trance.

The one thing which remains to be said about Poe's buildings is that cellars or catacombs, whenever they appear, stand for the irrational part of the mind; and that is so conventional an equation in symbolic literature that I think I need not be persuasive or illustrative about it. I had hoped, at this point, to discuss in a leisurely way some of the stories in which Poe makes use of his architectural properties, treating those stories as narrative wholes. But I have spoken too long about other things; and so, if you will allow me a few minutes more, I shall close by commenting briskly on two or three stories only.

The typical Poe story occurs *within* the mind of a poet; and its characters are not independent personalities, but allegorical figures representing the warring principles of the poet's divided nature. The lady Ligeia, for example, stands for that heavenly beauty which the poet's soul desires; while Rowena stands for that earthly, physical beauty which tempts the poet's passions. The action of the story is the dreaming soul's gradual emancipation from earthly attachments—which is allegorically expressed in the slow dissolution of Rowena. The result of this process is the soul's final, momentary vision of the heavenly Ligeia. Poe's typical story presents some such struggle between the visionary and the mundane; and the duration of Poe's typical story is the duration of a dream.

There are two tales in which Poe makes an especially clear and simple use of his architectural symbolism. The first is an unfamiliar tale called "The System of Dr. Tarr and Prof. Fether," and the edifice of that tale is a remote and dilapidated madhouse in southern France. What happens, in brief, is that the inmates of the madhouse escape from their cells in the basement of the building, overpower their keepers, and lock them up in their own cells. Having done this, the lunatics take possession of the upper reaches of the house. They shutter all the windows, put on odd costumes, and proceed to hold an uproarious and discordant feast, during which there is much eating and drinking of a disgusting kind, and a degraded version of Ligeia or Helen does a strip tease. At the height of these festivities, the keepers escape from their cells, break in through the barred and shuttered windows of the dining room, and restore order.

Well: the madhouse, like all of Poe's houses, is a mind. The keepers are the rational part of that mind, and the inmates are its irrational part. As you noticed, the irrational is suitably assigned to the cellar. The uprising of the inmates, and the suppression of the keepers, symbolizes the beginning of a dream, and the mad banquet which follows is perhaps Poe's least spiritual portrayal of the dream state: *this* dream, far from being an escape from the physical, consists exclusively of the release of animal appetites—as dreams sometimes do. When the keepers break in the windows, and subdue the revellers, they bring with them reason and the light of day, and the wild dream is over.

"The Masque of the Red Death" is a better-known and even more obvious example of architectural allegory. You will recall how Prince Prospero, when his dominions are being ravaged by the plague, withdraws with a thousand of his knights and ladies into a secluded, impregnable and window-less abbey, where after a time he entertains his friends with a costume ball. The weird décor of the seven ballrooms expresses the Prince's own taste, and in strange costumes of the Prince's own design the company dances far into the night, looking, as Poe says, like "a multitude of dreams." The festivities are interrupted only by the hourly striking of a gigantic ebony clock which stands in the westernmost room; and the striking of this clock has invariably a sobering effect on the revellers. Upon the last stroke of twelve, as you will remember, there appears amid the throng a figure attired in the blood-dabbled graveclothes of a plague-victim. The dancers shrink from him in terror. But the Prince, infuriated at what he takes to be an insolent practical joke, draws his dagger and pursues the figure through all of the seven rooms. In the last and westernmost room, the figure suddenly turns and confronts Prince Prospero, who gives a cry of despair and falls upon his own dagger. The Prince's friends rush forward to seize the intruder, who stands now within the shadow of the ebony clock; but they find nothing there. And then, one after the other, the thousand revellers fall dead of the Red Death, and the lights flicker out, and Prince Prospero's ball is at an end.

In spite of its cast of one thousand and two, "The Masque of the Red Death" has only one character. Prince Prospero is one-half of that character, the visionary half; the nameless figure in graveclothes is the other, as we shall see in a moment.

More than once, in his dialogues or critical writings, Poe describes the earth-bound, time-bound rationalism of his age as a *disease*. And that is what the Red Death signifies. Prince Prospero's flight from the Red Death is the poetic imagination's flight from temporal and worldly consciousness into dream. The thousand dancers of Prince Prospero's costume ball are just what Poe says they are—"dreams" or "phantasms," veiled and vivid creatures of Prince Prospero's rapt imagination. Whenever there is a feast, or carnival, or costume ball in Poe, we may be sure that a dream is in progress.

But what is the gigantic ebony clock? For the answer to that, one need only consult a dictionary of slang: we call the human heart a *ticker*, meaning that it is the clock of the body; and that is what Poe means here. In sleep, our minds may roam beyond the temporal world, but our hearts tick on, binding us to time and mortality. Whenever the ebony clock strikes, the dancers of Prince Prospero's dream grow momentarily pale and still, in half-awareness that they and their revel must have an end; it is as if a sleeper should half-awaken, and know that he has been dreaming, and then sink back into dreams again.

The figure in blood-dabbled graveclothes, who stalks through the terrified company and vanishes in the shadow of the clock, is waking temporal consciousness, and his coming means the death of dreams. He breaks up Prince Prospero's ball as the keepers in "Dr. Tarr and Prof. Fether" break up the revels of the lunatics. The final confrontation between Prince Prospero and the shrouded figure is like the terrible final meeting between William Wilson and his double. Recognizing his adversary as his own worldly and mortal self, Prince Prospero gives a cry of despair which is also Poe's cry of despair: despair at the realization that only by self-destruction could the poet fully free his soul from the trammels of this world.

Poe's aesthetic, Poe's theory of the nature of art, seems to me insane. To say that art should repudiate everything human and earthly, and find its subject matter at the flickering end of dreams, is hopelessly to narrow the scope and function of art. Poe's aesthetic points toward such impoverishments as *poésie pure* and the asbract expressionist movement in painting. And yet, despite his aesthetic, Poe is a great artist, and I would rest my case for him on his prose allegories of psychic conflict. In them, Poe broke wholly new ground, and they remain the best things of their kind in our literature. Poe's mind may have been a strange one; yet all minds are alike in their general structure; therefore we can understand him, and I think that he will have something to say to us as long as there is civil war in the palaces of men's minds.

CLARK GRIFFITH

Poe's "Ligeia" and the English Romantics

More than any of his major American contemporaries, Edgar Allan Poe shifted facilely and readily from one vein of prose fiction directly into another. There simply were no well-defined stages in Poe's writing, no set periods during which he concentrated exclusively upon some particular aspect of his prose material. Even the early, abortive Folio Club project was designed for a combination of humorous sketches and Gothic tales. And later as Poe's interests broadened to include satire, philosophy, and ratiocinative themes, he proved quite capable of composing, all within the space of a few months, a characteristic horror story, a burlesque, an analytical tale, and a metaphysical dialogue.

Yet it is a curious fact that critical studies of Poe regularly ignore the chronological pattern of his work and emphasize instead its similarities according to type. One can find a dozen worth-while books or essays in which scattered examples of Poe's fiction, individual pieces done ten or fifteen years apart, are lumped together in breathlessly neat categories. But one looks in vain for an interpreter who acknowledges that, however apparently different the actual texts may be, what Poe wrote in a given June was just possibly influenced by—was somehow interrelated with—what he had already written in the preceding May. The results of this overcompartmentalized approach are, I think, lamentable. Not only does study always by type but never by time destroy all sense of the continuity in Poe's writing. Much more seriously, it completely blinds us to whatever possibility there is that his scrambled order of composition, his easy hopping from genre to genre, may

From *University of Toronto Quarterly* 24 (1954). Copyright © 1954 by University of Toronto Press.

sometimes have been shrewdly purposeful—and may sometimes be most astonishingly revealing.

By way then of exploring certain potentialities latent in a chronological rather than typal investigation of Poe, let us consider "Ligeia" (1838). . . . "Ligeia" *is* what perceptive critics ranging from Philip Pendleton Cooke to Allen Tate have always called it, a gripping horror story, successfully rescued from the triteness of its kind by Poe's painstaking craftsmanship. It is, to be sure; and yet as one reads and re-reads the narrative, certain troublesome features persistently intrude. Problems of tone and symbolism, of characterization and, above all, of style, they never for a moment suggest that "Ligeia" is not a piece of Gothic fiction. . . . What they do imply is that close and searching scrutiny should make us the more wary of accepting it as simply a tale of terror, and as a text in which Gothic devices constitute the sole level of meaning. . . .

The first version of "Ligeia" appeared in the September, 1838, issue of the *American Museum of Literature and the Arts*. During this same year, Poe published only two other prose pieces, "Siope—A Fable," written (probably sometime late in 1837) for the January *Baltimore Book*, and "Psyche Zenobia," a burlesque which also appeared in the *American Museum*, just two months after "Ligeia." Both are obvious satires; and although they approach them quite differently, both satirize identical subjects . . .

"Siope" [is] a ruthless parody of Transcendentalism; "Psyche Zenobia," a merciless burlesque of Transcendental and Gothic writing; and between them [stands] the "Ligeia." At first glance, certainly, such a combination appears to do little more than underscore both the variety and the incredible unevenness in Poe's creative methods. Reading "Ligeia" as a straightforward tale of terror and turning then to the satires, one is readily persuaded that Poe himself drifted aimlessly—somewhat too aimlessly—from arrant nonsense into fiction of a high order into a realm of petty drivel, and that under the circumstances this is the only plausible deduction. Still, our initial examination of "Ligeia" unearthed several problems which the conventional approach did not seem fitted to solve. And when, with these matters brought to the foreground, the three pieces are read in the order of their publication, parallels or unexpected possibilities for parallels abruptly crystallize.

For one thing, it quickly becomes apparent that both "Siope" with its Gothic background plus its inarguable irony and "Psyche Zenobia" with its strange synthesis of *bizarrerie* and *intensity* ought to make us doubly sceptical of another tale of terror which contains any sort of questionable leavening. If Poe could play a trick once, he could likewise perform it twice; if he could theorize about a combination of Gothic *clichés* and Transcendental gibberish, he could also put theory into practice. But this is far from being all. "Siope" with its lush prose and "Psyche Zenobia" with its sardonic commentary on philosophical styles to be emphasized in terrifying situations should prompt us to look cautiously at other passages where Poe's language is a shade too full, a trace too mystical or metaphysical. And there is more. Just as "Siope" might well put us on guard for other references to opium dreams and Transcendentalism, just so "Psyche Zenobia" should alert us to another text in which Transcendentalism, Germany, England, indeed a kind of international motif figure large though ambiguously. And still more. Both implicitly and explicitly "Ligeia" *does* share qualities of the satires. Slight though it is, the allegorical method in "Psyche Zenobia" reminds us that "Ligeia" too is allegory. The pursuits ascribed to the lady Ligeia prefigure Mr. Blackwood's precepts. In "Ligeia" there are certain words and phrases which relate backward to "Siope," look ahead to "Psyche Zenobia."

. . . The burlesques published before and after "Ligeia" illuminate certain difficult aspects of "Ligeia" precisely because "Ligeia" is partly burlesque. Like "Siope," its predecessor, it combines Gothic overplot with satiric underside. Full of terror and sentiment but also of metaphysics and erudition, it duplicates the ideal horror story delineated in "Psyche Zenobia," its sequel. It is, in a word, an allegory of terror, almost perfectly co-ordinated with the subtlest of allegorized jests. . . .

In the surface-allegory, the lady Ligeia stands for mystery and madness, for an inflexible will to live, and for symbolic unreason. In the allegorized jest, her meanings are tailored to exemplify the mystery of a particular form of madness.

She was of a German background. Her studies "were more than all else adapted to deaden impressions of the outward world." The narrator felt her "rare learning" and "enthralling eloquence" creep into his heart by paces "steadily and stealthily progressive." Often, he remained unaware of her presence except as a "low sweet voice" drifting through his closed study. Ligeia's beauty "was the radiance of an opium dream"; and—in words lifted directly out of "Siope"—it was a vision more wildly divine "than the phantasies which hovered about the slumbering souls of the daughters of Delos." Additionally, her physical appearance shared the luxuriant grace of the Hebrews and the majestic spirituality of the Greeks.

Ligeia's eyes were the seat of a profound spirituality. During moments of "intense excitement," the "luminous orbs" acquired a beauty wholly distinct "from the formation, or the color, or the brilliancy of the features." At such times, their "*expression*" was of supreme importance, for it became rich with a metaphysical allusiveness, reflected back to the narrator "the beauty of beings either above or apart from the earth." Yet there was something immoderately singular about Ligeia's *"expression."* Ineffable and inscrutable, it resembled Mr. Blackwood's "tone mystic," hinting much but asserting nothing. Even for the narrator, who sought after complete understanding, the *"expression"* represented a "word of no meaning"; like *Silence* ("which is the merest word of all"), *"expression"* was a "vast latitude of mere sound [behind which] we entrench our ignorance of so much of the spiritual." But if Ligeia's profoundest glances were themselves unknowable, they did reproduce faint traces of their spirituality in an endless circle of known analogies—in "the commonest objects of the universe" and in "many existences in the material world."

Ligeia's intellect was immense. An *"intensity* in thought" set her apart from all others; and her learning, "gigantic" and "astounding," fanned out in every direction, came at last to encompass every conceivable area of knowledge. She was deeply proficient "in the classical tongues" and in all the "modern dialects of Europe." (Recall how the benefits of "'French, Spanish, Italian, German, Latin, and Greek'" were to be impressed upon Psyche Zenobia.) Her mastery extended over all "the most admired, because simply the most abstruse of the boasted erudition of the academy." ("'Talk of the academy and the lyceum,'" Psyche Zenobia would soon be counselled.) With astonishing ease, she traversed "*all* the wide areas of moral, natural, and mathematical science." (Psyche Zenobia was to hear much of Fichte, Kant, and Bossarion.) She guided the narrator, a child by contrast, through the "chaotic world of metaphysical investigation." (The schools Italic and Ionic, the terms *a priori* and *a posteriori* were to be important parts of Psyche Zenobia's education.) And then comes the key comment which lends both point and purpose to this altogether ludicrous account of Ligeia. Her "presence, her readings alone, rendered vividly luminous the many mysteries of . . . transcendentalism." Ligeia was a Transcendentalist.

She symbolizes, in sober fact, the very incarnation of German idealism, German Transcendentalism provided with an allegorical form. First suggested by her nationality and mystical behaviour and subjectivistic studies, her role in the satire is further betrayed by the meaningless meaning of her strangely metaphysical eyes. It is reemphasized by her spiritual glances, unintelligible except for their reappearance in material existences. It is rounded out by her "intensities," her personification of just the qualities Psyche Zenobia would presently be urged to cultivate, her elucidation of Transcendental mysteries. If, however, additional evidence seems desirable, it can easily be drawn from the narrator's attitude toward and his relationship with Ligeia.

In the Gothic overplot, the narrator is pictured as a psychopath, as a bereaved husband, and as the recording consciousness, shattered by the

anomalies it perceives. In the satiric underside of "Ligeia," his lunacy becomes the lunacy of a confirmed "Crazyite."

The narrator was Ligeia's student in the sense that the dark lady was
his teacher. He was a student of Ligeia in the sense that she represented the
object of his studies. As the "unfathomable meaning of [Ligeia's] glance" sank
deeply into his soul, the narrator longed for larger understanding. Relent-
lessly, he pondered her expression. Throughout the "whole of a midsummer
night," he "struggled to fathom it." What was it, he never wearied of asking
himself, "What was it—that something more profound than the well of
Democritus—which lay far within the pupils of my beloved? What *was*
it? . . . Those eyes! those large, those shining, those divine orbs!" But when
no response was forthcoming, he temporarily abandoned all hopes for complete comprehension, and contented himself with "discovering in the commonest objects of the universe, a circle of analogies to that expression." He
recognized something of its spirituality in the

> survey of a rapidly growing vine—in the contemplation of a moth, a
> butterfly, a chrysalis, a stream of running water . . . in the ocean, in the
> falling of a meteor . . . in the glances of unusually aged people . . . [in] one or
> two stars . . . [in] certain sounds from stringed instruments . . . [in] passages
> from books . . . in a volume of Joseph Glanvill . . . : 'And the will therein
> lieth, which dieth not. Who knoweth the mysteries of the will, with its
> vigor? For God is but a great will pervading all things by nature of its
> intentness. Man doth not yield him to the angels utterly, save only through
> the weakness of his feeble will.'

Of the dozen or so items in this list, only one—the so-called Glanvill
quotation—bears directly upon the overplot. For the rest, they simply suggest
that Poe is slyly mocking Ligeia's spiritual depths by comparing them to an
assortment of oddly incongruous details, by describing them in prose very like
the "tone heterogenous." And opening up this possibility, they instantly
remind one of the Transcendentalists who were likewise glimpsing spiritual
analogues in the "commonest objects of the universe," in such "'pertinent
and pretty'" places as nature, clothes-symbols, and the works of German
literature.

For the narrator, Ligeia posed an unsolved metaphysical riddle. But
mystified and entranced by her rare learning, he confidently assumed that she
herself would ultimately unravel the puzzle which she herself symbolized.
Humbly aware of her "infinite supremacy," he pursued like an eager child the
obscure import of her teachings. And, as he expresses it,

> With how vast a triumph—with how vivid a delight—with how much of all
> that is ethereal in hope—did I *feel*, as she bent over me, in studies but little
> sought for—but less known that delicious vista by slow but very perceptible

degrees expanding before me, down whose long, gorgeous, and all untrod-
den path I might at length pass onward to the goal of a wisdom too divinely
precious not to be forbidden.

Then, as before, there comes the final comment, justifying this fantastic, this
almost obscene overwriting. At the foot of the path lay full mastery of the
"many mysteries of the transcendentalism" in which the narrator was im-
mersed. By first portraying himself as the student of Ligeia and next as the
student of Transcendentalism, by passing at once from the many mysteries of
Ligeia to the many mysteries of Transcendentalism, Poe's spokesman has
confirmed the dark lady's place in the satire—and thereby disclosed his own.

Actually two things are fundamentally dubious about the narrator's
reference to Transcendental pursuits. Although Poe's tales of terror frequently picture the human mind in its gradual advance upon esoteric knowledge, the exact nature of the new discovery is seldom, if ever, divulged. In
"Ms. Found in a Bottle" or "The Fall of the House of Usher," no character
can even visualize, much less define, the awful mysteries for which he is
compelled to search; their vagueness is an indispensable adjunct to the
supernaturalism in the story. Here, by contrast, the object of the intellectual
quest is not merely named. It is explicitly embodied in another character and,
what is yet more suspect, it is given the selfsame label Poe had already flayed
once and would flay again in the year 1838. Surely, these facts are of overriding
significance: surely, they contribute all the proof needed to identify the
narrator as a prototype of Poe's favourite whipping-boy, the Transcendentalist who speaks the language of a *Blackwood's intensity*, who looks into the
"nature of affairs a very great deal farther than anybody else," and whose
intellectual pretensions are bolstered by gleanings from the German.

Ligeia died; and her death, her fierce struggles, and grim wrestlings
with the shadow belong to the Gothic overplot. The narrator's reaction,
however, is a different matter. Recounting Ligeia's fatal illness, he makes it
clear that his chief bereavement was the loss of her informing glances. When
her eyes, at once the symbol of the Transcendental puzzle and the avenue to
its resolution, shone "less and less frequently upon the pages over which [he]
pored," the narrator's despair knew no bounds. Wanting the "radiant luster"
of those eyes, he cries in an agony of grief, "letters, lambent and golden, grew
duller than Saturnian lead." Not simply letters, but golden letters; this, as it
happens, is the initial allusion to gold, one of the two basic colours in Poe's
allegory.

Other gold-images quickly accumulate once the narrator arrives in
England. England itself is "fair." Rowena Trevanion of Tremaine is "fair-
haired." The accoutrements of the narrator's English estate include gold
carpets, golden candelabra, gold tapestries and ottomans, chains and pen-

dants of solid gold. Yet despite the garish splendour of all these objects, none are permitted to shine with a pure golden radiance. Across one wall of the apartment where they were located and where the narrator dwelt with Rowena, there ran a single windowpane. It was "an immense sheet of unbroken glass . . . and tinted of a leaden hue, so that the rays of either sun or moon, passing through it, fell with a ghastly luster on the objects within." Now there is, to be sure, nothing inherently peculiar in such a window; it is sinister-looking and blends sufficiently well into the Gothic backdrop. Nevertheless, its appearance in this context does balance out a curious parallel. In effect, Poe has transferred to Rowena and to the English *mise en scène* the same leaden dullness which overspread the golden letters of Transcendentalism when the German Ligeia could no longer gloss and enrich their inmost meanings.

As we have noticed, several features connected with the abbey, with Rowena, and with the narrator's behaviour in fair England are not readily assimilable into the surface allegory. But if, as seems likely, Poe's colour scheme is less a matter of coincidence than of malicious design, these apparent inanities merge in the allegorized satire and become the cream of the jest.

The abbey was situated in one of "the wildest and least frequented portions of fair England," in a region notoriously "remote and unsocial." Surrounded by "gloomy" and "dreary grandeur," overhung with "mossy" ruin, "aged vine," and "verdant decay," the external building faced upon a "savage domain." Within, were "melancholy and time-honored memories," castellated turrets, ceilings "excessively lofty, vaulted, and elaborately fretted with the wildest and most grotesque specimens of a semi-Gothic, semi-druidical device." Clearly enough, this reads much like a typical Poe setting. But the trouble is that it typifies, almost too perfectly, the whole of an intellectual-aesthetic era as well. Swamped by a welter of Romantic *clichés* and perceiving how each is quite uncharacteristically pinned down to a specific geographical locale, we suspect that the English abbey, like the lady Ligeia and Mr. Blackwood's editorial rooms, is less a traditional Poe-symbol than a merely traditional symbol, exposed here to Poe's acid parody. The abbey could be—and, in point of fact, there is abundant evidence for stating it is—a take-off on Scott's scenic effects, similarly, it could be interpreted as Poe's caricature of the desolate landscape at Craigenputtock or of the Lake Country and the "violet by the mossy stone."

Filling any or all of these roles, the abbey is brilliantly suited to its principal English occupant, the lady Rowena Trevanion of Tremaine. With her name drawn equally out of *Ivanhoe* and "Christabel," Rowena, we may fairly assume, is the living incarnation of English Romanticism, English

Romantic—or English Transcendental—thought cloaked in allegorical trappings. Yet in the narrator's view, the lady of Tremaine was as destitute of Ligeia's miraculous insights as of her stupendous learning and oracular gibberish. Conventional and dull, the blond was simply another of those golden objects overcast by the leaden-grey window. Only in a moment "of his mental alienation" did she seem to the narrator to be a fit "successor of the unforgotten Ligeia"; soon he came to loathe her "with a hatred belonging more to demon than to man." Rowena, in short, symbolizes an impoverished English Romanticism, as yet "unspiritualized" by German cant. Consequently, she represents but a shallow pretense of Romanticism; and—on this point the text is admirably plain—it is a part of Poe's joke to make her Romantic in nothing save her borrowed name.

Despising Rowena, abandoning himself to orgies of grief, the narrator increasingly revelled "(oh with what intensity of regret)" in recollections of Ligeia's "purity, of her wisdom, of her lofty, her ethereal nature." He perpetuated her memory in the lavish *décor* of his chambers. Appropriately, he invoked her spirit in nature, calling "aloud upon her name . . . among the sheltered recesses of the glens." Chiefly, however, he sought to recover her mystical being in the wild hallucinations engendered by opium. From the outset, we observed, he identified Ligeia's transcendent beauty with an opium dream, and early betrayed something of Poe's satiric intent by describing her in terms first used in "Siope." Now when his spirit most burned to unite with "all the fires of [Ligeia's] own," he was habitually fettered "in the shackles of the drug." As the author of *Confessions of an Opium-Eater* (in Poe's mind, Coleridge) deplored the dearth of English philosophy and boasted in the same breath of his opium feats and wide readings from the German, so Poe's narrator, contemptuous of the English Rowena, gave himself up to drugged visions of the German Ligeia. The very decorations, where emblems of Ligeia's dark spirituality were scattered across Rowena's grey-gold dullness, took their "colouring from [his] dreams." Excited by opium, he shrieked Ligeia's name "during the silences of the night." In a drugged frenzy, he glimpsed her mystical shadow, and felt his "whole soul was awakened within." Opium and Ligeia were inseparable; together with nature, the narcotic became a means of restoring the dark lady "to the pathways she had abandoned upon earth."

But there is, to repeat, no satisfactory reason why the narrator's addiction should appear in the Gothic overplot. Inevitably, it weakens the climax of the tale, suggesting that what the narrator finally beholds is more delusion than objective circumstance. Hence it goes far toward vitiating the drama of Ligeia's restoration—unless, of course, that restoration is susceptible to a second interpretation.

When Poe's friend and critic Philip Pendleton Cooke examined the first published version of "Ligeia," he complained of only one major defect. For the sake of fuller credibility, he insisted, the conclusion should have been somewhat modified. The completed transition from Rowena to Ligeia was a "violation of the ghostly proprieties"; a reader would be shocked into unbelief upon discovering how a "wandering essence . . . could, *in quickening the body of the Lady Rowena* (such is the idea) become suddenly the visible, bodily, Ligeia." Poe made great show of agreeing. "Touching Ligeia," he replied, "you are right—all right—throughout. . . . I should have intimated that the *will* did not perfect its intention—there should have been a relapse—a final one—and Ligeia should be at length entombed as Rowena—the bodily alterations having gradually faded away." Yet the fact remains that twice during the next seven years "Ligeia" underwent revisions extensive and slight; and on both occasions Poe left essentially unchanged the ending for which he had so profusely apologized. Did he retain the objectionable climax because, as he rather lamely (and for that matter, rather inaccurately) told Cooke, it differentiated between "Ligeia" and the earlier "Morella"? Or did he retain it because, hugely enjoying the second, secret meaning of his "wandering essence," he recognized that Ligeia's bodily conquest of Rowena was absolutely necessary for the satire? In view of all that has gone before and in terms of the conclusion itself, the latter alternative seems considerably more plausible.

For what, in its largest sense, does the "ghostly" transformation in "Ligeia" signify? Why, nothing less, really, than a dramatic enactment of what would become one of the most comic sections of "Psyche Zenobia." To the Signora—fretting because her Romantic compatriots lacked "profundity . . . reading . . . metaphysics . . . spirituality . . . cant . . . with a capital K," fretting because "there was no investigation of first causes, first principles . . . no attention paid to that great point the 'fitness of things'"—to this sorely tried lady, Mr. Blackwood would offer sage words of wisdom. Write many languages. Master metaphysics. Talk of the academy. Bring in the words *a priori* and *a posteriori*. Stress the Germans; above all, stress the Germans. Abuse Locke, but praise Fichte, Schelling and Kant. Make *The Sorrows of Werther* a by-word. Collectively, these are the pomposities which will reanimate the deadest of Romanticisms. Since it is Mr. Blackwood who compiles them, they are, manifestly, the generating root of English Romanticism itself. Symbolized in the lady Ligeia, they constitute the "chronic disease" and the "distemper of fancy" which topple Rowena's reason "from her throne." In turn, they become the vital forces which rejuvenate Rowena, dispel her clammy pallor, quicken her into new life—but re-shape her until she is unrecognizable except as Ligeia.

Here, then, at least, shrieks the narrator when his long vigil has been rewarded: "Here, then, at least . . . can I never—can I never be mistaken—these are the full, and the black, and the wild eyes of the lady—of the lady Ligeia." At the end, it is Ligeia's mystical *expression* which prevails. Reflecting a metaphysical beauty, discernible in nature and dreams, pondered by the student of Transcendentalism, this "vast latitude of mere sound" is Ligeia's link with German idealism. And now, the "word of no meaning" has left its ineffaceable stamp upon Rowena. In the allegorized jest, therefore, qualities fundamentally German do indeed take primacy over properties basically English. For Poe has compounded terror with satire, and the triumph of German sources over an English Romanticism, hopelessly uninspired without them, could hardly be more complete.

DANIEL HOFFMAN

The Marriage Group

'A SERIES OF MERE HOUSEHOLD EVENTS'

Edgar Poe is a prose-poet of love, an analyst and dramatist in his tales of the deepest of all attachments, the passion of a man for a woman. Recalling that this is the very emotion which, in 'Al Aaraaf,' barred the spirit Angelo from Heaven, it may come as a surprise to be told that Poe is a great love poet. In his prose. But it is so.

What he writes on this theme will not readily be confused with the efforts of others. For who besides Poe has so clearly felt (whether he consciously understood it or not is beside the point, so vividly is the feeling expressed in his tales), the intense symbiosis between love and hatred? Here, as everywhere, Edgarpoe looks into the dark glass of his soul, and sees doubly. His tales of courtship, marriage, and life in the resulting love nest are *something else* indeed from those of any writer before him. Few since have dared, or have sought the courage to dare, to look with so pitiless a gaze so deeply into their own souls. Love is seldom as simple or as happy as is popularly hoped. And Poe, who in these tales of love, courtship, and marriage, if nowhere else, fulfilled the behest described in his own *Marginalia*—to write a book called 'My Heart Laid Bare,' in which the *truth* be told—discovered ways to tell the nearly insupportable truths of his own soul. A soul in perpetual torment, for, as we shall see, its dispositions of feeling were such from birth—or from before birth—that there could have been no satisfactory fulfilment of its insatiable longings. Such, in outline, was the tragedy of Edgar Allan Poe. Such, in brief, is the human condition also, more or less, although, to be sure, most of us are enabled to transfer our attentions to the substitutes which this life offers for the impossible Archetypes of the erotic imagination. Yet does he not speak to our condition who cannot permit his imagination the freedom of such transference? Poe is a haunted man, haunted by the recrudescence, in daydream or in dream, of the spectral love-object whose image, imprinted on the proverbial film of the deepest reel in memory's storage-bank, neither life nor language can ever actually assuage. The ghost that will not be laid.

Because there may lurk such a ghost within us all, Poe, in his weird tales of love, plucks not only the wild chords of his own sufferings but also touches a universal heartstring. And so he explores the reciprocities between love and hatred, between the acceptance of another person as the actual fulfilment of an erotic ideal and *the need to destroy* that same person as the betrayal of the ideal with whom she has—by a horrible error, a fatal mistake of the lover's being—been so invested: this too is part of the love-knot tied and disentangled by that victim of Cupid, Edgar Poe. Not everybody's valentine, though Edgar offers 'The Black Cat,' one of his explorations of these emotions, as 'a series of mere household events.' Yet even this matter-of-fact narrator calls his narrative 'the most wild yet most homely,' and assures us that he is not mad. These things may seem beyond belief, he says, but,

> Hereafter, perhaps, some intellect may be found which will reduce my phantasm to the commonplace—some intellect more calm, more logical, and far less excitable than my own, which will perceive, in the circum-stances I detail with awe, nothing more than an ordinary succession of very natural causes and effects.

In short, however grotesque are the elements in the design of the ensuing Arabesque, they will declare themselves in an intelligible order to a ratiocinative mind of sufficient power.

Once again we are faced with a problem in detection. As in 'The Murders in the Rue Morgue,' the crime is the murder of a woman. And, as in 'The Purloined Letter,' the culprit is identified from the start. The problem here is, from his confession *to deduce his motive.*

The narrator of 'The Black Cat' is a husband, yet his wife is never named. It is as though she has no name, or he cannot remember it, or he dare not speak it. Nearly everywhere else we have seen Poe bestow upon the beloveds, fiancées, and brides of his poems and tales the most euphonious and original cognomens: Eulalie, Ulalume, Helen, Annabel Lee, Ligeia, Morella, Madeline, Berenice. But this wife has no name.

It is she who suggests, to the narrator who is so tender toward his pets, the old superstition that a black cat is a witch in disguise. As in 'The Tell-Tale Heart,' where the belief in the Evil Eye is introduced to make more spooky the power of the old man's gaze, here too folklore is pressed into the service of Poe's plot. Wife suggests, but husband may in truth believe, that black cat=witch. This, and other evidence soon to be introduced and offered in the present brief, lead me to suggest that, in the synoptic and evasive glossary of this tale, witch=wife. Ergo, black cat=wife.

In this story we are told all about the narrator's feelings—first of affection, then of loathing—for his cat, but of his attitude to or relations with his wife we learn next to nothing. The relation with the cat begins as mutual love, the cat (Pluto by name) cuddling up against him, he petting and fondling Pluto. Then the demon of intemperance (the Imp of the Perverse disguised as the Angel of the Odd) takes possession of the man. He becomes a drunkard, he curses his wife, he strikes her, and gradually he conceives absolute detestation of the affectionate cat. Becoming panicky at his unpredictable behavior, the cat bites his hand. Now enraged, he seizes the poor thing and with his penknife carves out one of its eyes.

Even for so horrible a misdeed he feels, when sober, inadequate remorse. The awful wound heals, and the cat, as before, continues to seek his companionship. His disgust and loathing grow. He can stand its importunities no longer—he hangs the creature by the neck, from a tree in the garden—'hung it *because* I knew that it had loved me, and *because* I felt it had given me no reason of offence.'

That very night his house goes up in flames. All is destroyed save one wall, and on that wall, newly plastered, is imprinted by fire the image of the cat hanging from its noose. The narrator is much surprised by this graphic preservation of the crime which he forbears to cite as the cause of his disaster. He figures out an unlikely rational explanation for this phenomenon (the details of which are irrelevant to my purpose here).

This would seem to be the whole story of the black cat. But no, in the manner of dreams which haunt the dreamer over again, there is a recrudescence of the black cat—the narrator becomes aware, in a gin mill one night, of *another* black cat, sitting atop a barrel, whose provenience no one knows. This creature attaches itself *to him*, follows him home, and he becomes aware that it is the spitting image of Pluto, even to its lacking one eye. His wife is delighted with the new cat, but he notices that a splotch of white hair on its breast grows in time to resemble the outline of a *gallows*. Pluto habitually climbs, claws embedded in its master's clothing, 'to my breast.' 'At such times,' he says, 'although I longed to destroy it with one blow, I was yet withheld from so doing . . . by absolute *dread* of the beast.'

One day, with his wife he goes down the steep cellar stairs on some errand. The cat follows, nearly tripping him headlong. In exasperation he grabs an axe and raises it, 'forgetting in my wrath the childish dread . . .' His wife impulsively tries to stay his hand (her Imp of the Perverse?). 'Goaded by this interference into a rage more than demoniacal, I withdrew my arm from her grasp and buried the axe in her brain.' (His.) 'She fell dead upon the spot without a groan.'

Is narrator overcome with remorse, prostrated with grief? Does he weep, does he lament the terrible accident? Not at all. 'This hideous murder accomplished, I set myself forthwith, and with entire deliberation, to the task of concealing the body.' This hideous *murder!* As though he can now admit it had been his unacknowledged purpose all along. How more plainly, without violating the dynamics of his tale, could Poe have told us that from the first the cat had been but a displacement of the wife! Now the murderer, methodical as the madman who smothered the old fellow with the ever-watchful eye, must contrive to dispose of the body. As had that other youth, he considers 'cutting the corpse into minute fragments'; like him, this murderer also thinks of putting the parts beneath the floorboards. But no, he chooses intead (like Montresor) 'to wall it up in the cellar.' And this he neatly does. Now he notices that the cat is nowhere to be seen.

> It is impossible to describe, or to imagine, the deep, the blissful sense of relief which the absence of the detested creature occasioned in my bosom. It did not make its appearance during the night.

Which creature? Is it the cat whose absence by night delights his bosom with blissful relief? Not a word does he say of his feelings at the simultaneous disappearance from his bed and bosom of his wife. Well may we understand the tranquillity of this narrator's sleep when with one blow he has removed from his life both the real and the surrogate source of his terror.

Let us leave him sleeping blissfully for the moment, while we consider some curious features of this 'series of mere household events.' A frightened cat would be likely to scratch its owner, but narrator is goaded to cut out its eye not by a scratch but by a *bite*. But see, there's more to chew on here than at first glance appeared. As Mme Bonaparte intuited, identifying the cat's mouth as the feared *vagina dentata*. Very good, and not as absurdly unlikely as may at first appear. Let me expatiate a moment on teeth and mouths, eyes and other members, as we meet them and the narrators who are fixated upon them in Poe's tales. I got to thinking, why did this narrator wait until the cat bit him, rather than go into his tantrum when scratched?

The answer may be right before my eyes, but I've become so arduous a Poe-taster that I can't help but follow a slightly devious chain of clues. There is another of Eddie's love stories in which much is made of teeth, the teeth of Berenice, who, as was true of Poe's own wife, Virginia, is the cousin of the poor fellow who tells their tale. Egaeus, her fiancé, says, 'Of Berenice I . . . seriously believed *que tous ses dents étaient des idées. Des idées!* . . . ah, *therefore* it was that I coveted them so madly.' This seems kinky in the extreme, *particularly* when he violates the poor girl's grave to rip the teeth from her mouth. But isn't this fetish of the unfortunate Egaeus rather like that of Ligeia's husband for that lady's *eyes*? As Egaeus describes the presentiment by which he first becomes fixated upon the teeth of Berenice we see the correspondence between these features further explicated:

> The eyes were lifeless and lustreless, and seemingly pupilless, and I shrank involuntarily from their glassy stare to the contemplation of the thin and shrunken lips. . . . The teeth!—the teeth!—they were here and there, and everywhere, visibly and palpably before me; long, narrow, and excessively white, with the pale lips writhing about them.

And these teeth represent *des idées*. Now the mouth is not usually thought of as an *intellectual* organ, while the eye conventionally has this designation. Still, when we wish to say that we comprehend something, we may say we have digested it, or chewed it over, or ruminated thereon. But the weird images in Poe's love tales reach below the level of linguistic formation to establish the similitudes they make of certain bodily parts.

Consider in what ways mouth and eye resemble each other. Each is an orifice in the body, surrounded by lips or lids which seem to open and close by a will of their own. Each is lubricated with a fluid of its own origin, and each leads inward—toward the stomach, toward the brain, toward the mysterious interior of the living creature. The thought may occur which other orifice of the body—of the female body—these two, in the respects just mentioned, might be conceived to resemble. And let us propose, for the purposes of this investigation, a male ratiocinator who is rendered incapable of referring to, of dealing with, of describing, of touching, that female part—rendered so by a fear, a terror, a hysteria so pervading that he must obsessively dwell on what he cannot bring himself to touch. How then can he respond to his inescapable need? The human being is a devious creature. Imagination can offer substitutes for the forbidden fruit. Poe's narrators are compelled to see, to bite and taste, that forbidden fruit, not aware of what it is. This is not to say that the reader (and perhaps even the author, at that level of deep awareness at which he exercises artistic control over his fantasies) is not aware. Maybe our awareness remains mostly subliminal. At any rate these terrible tales touch some deep resonance in us, or we should not read them at all.

So complete is the working-out of these strange similitudes, these symbolic substitutions, in Edgar Poe's imagination that when he exercises artistic control upon the obsessive materials a whole set of related correspondences come into play. *Ses dents étaient des idées* . . . Just as the vagina is the entrance to the mysterious womb, the unifier of all life, so is the eye to that all-synthesizing ratiocinator, the brain; and the teeth to the all-digesting stomach, in which the womb is lodged. And now, perhaps, the bizarre intellectualization of the courtship of the Poetagonists—the mental giganticism attributed by them to Morella and Ligeia—comes clear.

For reasons we are still attempting to fathom, Poe was never able directly to treat of his obsessive longing to be reborn in the womb, the re-entrance into which becomes, as a result of his terror, an image of death, so that prenatal bliss and life after death are images of one another. Images of that primary unity to which the soul tends, for which it agonizingly pines. Let me not equivocate, the reason for this evasion, for its repression and sublimation is everywhere evident. Such thoughts as these cut too close to the bone, they verge all too closely upon the forbidden lust of the id—the lust the ego usually rejects and tries to repress and control—for its own maternal original, the interuterine life before birth. Therefore this longing is everywhere disguised. By shifting the object of fascination from the unmentionable and terrifying vagina to the mouth or the eye, and by substituting for the attributes of the unifying womb those of the unifying mind, Poe is able to pursue, in masquerade and charade, the object, and the consequences, of his obsessional love-attachment.

So when the narrator undertakes to do injury to the hitherto inoffensive cat, he repays its having given him a little bite—by cutting out its eye. The bite, the bite . . . given by the creature in fear . . . might this not be a hysterical and aggressive form of a caress? For indeed the mouth is an organ of caressing, and biting a means of erotic excitation. Eating one another. Isn't this excitation what the narrator of this household tale is so terribly afraid of? The removal of the offender's eye is clearly a substitute excision (in another disguise) of the same organ which terrifies him—the eye a substitute for the teeth, the teeth a substitute for the female part. This intricate series of substitutions enables us to be reminded of the most archaic code of *justice*. For such a crime the exaction must be an eye for an eye, a tooth for a tooth.

The hanging of the black cat comes next. Princess Bonaparte considers the hung cat to be not in fact the victim of the impenitent narrator, but the penis of the impotent author. The cat is so emphatically a wife-substitute, though, that I find it difficult to think it at the same time a penis-substitute. I prefer to think that hanging can represent female impotence as well as male, and that Poe's mad narrator is displacing onto the surrogate for his wife, whose passion, whose clutching bites and embraces menace him, the impotence which he himself cannot escape.

With the appearance of the second cat we know we are in dream-land. The mark on its throat—a gallows—may be seen only by the narrator. The *lex talionis* is beginning to close its noose around his own throat. The whole tale, he tells us at the outset, is his gallows confession. He is about to be hanged. Then, indeed will *he* be impotent, like the cat.

Oh, the *dénouement*. As in 'The Tell-Tale Heart,' the blissful murderer's repose is interrupted by a clamor at the door. The police arrive. Once more the culprit invites them to tour the premises. Yet again he leads them to the very spot behind which is concealed the incriminating corpse. 'And here, through the mere frenzy of bravado, I rapped heavily with a cane . . . upon that very portion of the brickwork behind which stood the corpse of the wife of my bosom.' How audaciously does this fellow defy—or should we say invite—his fate!

> But may God shield and deliver me from the fangs of the Arch-Fiend! No sooner had the reverberation of my blows sunk into silence, than I was answered by a voice from within the tomb!

Strong arms rip down the plaster, and there, perched atop the head of the already rotted and erect corpse, 'with red extended mouth and solitary eye of fire, sat the hideous beast whose craft had seduced me into murder, and whose informing voice had consigned me to the hangman.' Tooth and eye, eye and tooth. The concentric circle of this man's fate has tightened in the noose around his neck—yet another terrifying image of that which in his imagination has been represented by mouth, teeth, eye-socket, and eye. An "I" for an eye.

AVERSIONS

Think not that Edgar is so terrified of nuptials that he cannot joke, in his fashion, on this head. The maidenhead. Where his nightmarish tales of murdering the beloved '*because* I knew that it had loved me' are terse with the economy of a pefectly calculated symbolism, his knockabout burlesques and farces are prolix. The narrators of these Grotesques like to laugh and laugh, or try to make us do likewise, for as long as someone is laughing they do not have to surrender to the hysteria their comical predicaments disguise.

Take the case of the youth in 'The Spectacles,' a Grotesque on that most romantic subject, courtship, or rather, love at first sight. Simpson, as he calls himself though of French descent, having changed his name to gain an inheritance, is only twenty-two, handsome, well-apportioned, but he has very weak *eyes*. Indeed he can scarcely see. But vanity precludes his wearing glasses. Therefore, from a distance—from his box at the opera—he beholds and is smitten by the ethereal beauty of a woman, Madame Lalande. I won't try to recapitulate the machinery of this rather tedious spoof; let it suffice that there are in fact two Mme Lalandes, and when Simpson's friends realize that he has set his heart not on the lithe young French woman but on her elder companion of the same name, they conspire with that lady to play a trick on the self-willed suitor. He pays assiduous court to this Mme Lalande, and she, surprisingly, requests that he vow to wear spectacles. He gallantly promises to do so, as a favor to her, after their wedding. As you can see, the stage is set to prove how blind is love.

After the midnight wedding, in their carriage, young Simpson, obedient to his vows, dons his glasses—and finds he has married a shrivelled old be-rouged, be-powdered, be-wigged and padded old woman of eighty-two. His bride is the female counterpart of The Man That Was Used Up! The body is a piece of machinery.

But that's not the end of Simpson's discomfiture. Replying to his expostulations, Mme Lalande—Mrs. Simpson—delivers herself of her genealogy and that of her descendants, and it comes to the young man that he has married his own great-great grandmother!

But keep on laughing, for the last paragraph resolves these embarrassments. The ceremony, like his courtship, has been a joke. His friends plotted it all, one of them impersonated the priest, so the wedding was no wedding. And the finale brings this near-sighted lover a bliss perhaps beyond his deserts: he gets to marry the other Mme Lalande, the *really* young, really beautiful companion of her great aunt of the same name.

So he doesn't have to marry his great-great grandmother. He marries his cousin. Even if we smile at Poe's impostures, aren't we struck by the consanguinity which afflicts his suitor? How curious that his faulty vision leads so precipitously toward incest! And the happy resolution only mitigates somewhat the closeness of the attachment of his heart for a member of his mother's blood.

A cousin, not so many times removed as is Mme Lalande from Simpson, is the object of desire for the suitor named Egaeus, he of the fixation upon the teeth of Berenice. The tale that bears her name is an Arabesque whose terror complements the jocose knockabout of 'The Spectacles.' Egaeus and Berenice never know their nuptial day, for the lady falls sick, wastes away, and on a certain black day is found apparently dead. No time is lost in hurrying her body to its tomb. It is on that night that her now demented lover, acting in a trance, violates her grave—he remembers shrieks—and awakens when a horrified servant tells him of the spoliation of Berenice's tomb—something about her being *still alive* when the teeth were ripped from her mouth.

The disease which afflicted Berenice at first appeared to be the consumption to which Poe's ladies are so vulnerable, but her final fit nonetheless proved an epileptic seizure. As was so comically foretold in 'The Premature Burial.' Like the husband of 'The Black Cat,' Egaeus has murdered the one who loved him most—and has pulled the teeth from the mouth whose writhing lips obsessed him.

Nightmare horror and death thus cheat Berenice and Egaeus of the peaceful consummation of their love. In fact we have yet to follow one of

Poe's suitors to the marriage bed. (I leave out of account the pillow talk of the nameless wife and husband in 'The Black Cat.') What, for Poe-people, is life like after the wedding? That is the burden of another of his hilarious comedies, 'Loss of Breath.'

Hilarious because the husband discovers, on the morning after their wedding, as he launches a string of vilifications against his new bride, that he cannot speak them—because he has lost his breath. Not for nothing is his name Mr. Lackobreath. Nor should we be surprised that he discovers, among his wife's effects (in which he searches *for his lost breath*) 'a number of *billets doux* from Mr. Windenough.' He also finds 'a set of false teeth, two pairs of hips, an eye.' Alas, it appears Mr. Lackobreath has married the wrong Mme Lalande after all.

Is there any meaning to this laborious jocosity? It is well established that, on the oneiric level of conceptualization, which Poe seems to have had accessible to his imagination almost at will, whether he committed himself to the Arabesque or the Grotesque mode, ability to breathe is interchangeably connected with sexual potency. It is quite clear from the details of Poe's sketch that Mr. Lackobreath has had his ability to breathe taken from him on his nuptial night. Mr. Windenough would seem able to breathe with ease, with impunity. For a dozen frenzied pages Mr. Lackobreath suffers the consequences of his loss—he is taken for dead; he is disfigured, his nose and ears are cut off (as though loss of breath weren't sufficient a symbolization of what ails him), he is crushed, battered, and at last—what else should we expect?—put in the tomb while conscious still, though still out of breath. He seems to enjoy his premature inhumation, especially when he discovers that the vault also contains his rival. This tale runs itself into the ground and isn't really very funny; Lackobreath exacts some breath from Windenough, they at length are liberated from the tomb—but the curious part is, there's no further word in the story about Mrs. Lackobreath. She drops out of sight, out of mind, and the tale concludes with some of Funny Edgar's dreary comicality in the pompous, philosophical line. In short, hysteria takes over and the source of the difficulty is quite repressed. Regaining his ability to breathe, Lackobreath is content with that literal power. It is as though speech, talk talk talk were all the potency he desires. Like Montresor, he cannot stop himself from telling his tale.

I HAVE BEEN FAITHFUL TO YOU IN MY FASHION

The very thought of a consummated marriage struck Poe's imagination with terror. As is plain from 'The Spectacles' and 'Loss of Breath,' he was beset by redoubled fears of committing incest and of connubial non-performance—equally damned if he did and damned if he didn't. Poor Edgar responded by aggressively exhibiting himself to the view of the curious world. But such self-exposures proved a sort of send-up, like his voyages to the moon and into the maelstrom. Appearing in motley, Edgar commits burlesques so broad that the object lampooned can't be the author at all, but some other poor forked carrot with no more human reality in him than has the butt of a joke.

Still, not all the stories in Edgar Poe's 'Marriage Group' are burlesques, the modern writer's approximation of fabliaux. No, these appear only in Poe's monogamous tales. When he contrives a plot involving not merely the marriage of a hapless Poetagonist but his *remarriage* also, then the gears, rods, and pistons of Poe's fictional *frisson*-machine shift from the bump and clatter of his Grotesques to the wilder, smoother rhythms of Arabesques. Then, then, his theme becomes too serious altogether for flummery or the release of fears in raucous laughter. Then, the fears are instead indulged, luxuriated in. They are savored, they are enjoyed.

Of the tales I have in mind, the finest and most fully articulated is surely 'Ligeia.' (Others include 'Morella' and 'Eleanora.' The theme itself was one Poe had early tried to use in poetry, producing only the bathetic 'Bridal Ballad.') And of all of Poe's tales 'Ligeia' has been among the most frequently examined and explained, though to be sure its explainers seem to me systematically to have missed the point of the story, being diverted by whatever system of thought they attempt to impose on it. Controversialists in the learned journals have savaged one another over such questions as whether 'Ligeia' is a tale of vampirism (drawing on the long roster of vampire fiction, legend, and belief) or a story of transmigration of souls (this involves the long history of soul-displacement in literature and fable). One scholar has recently proposed that in marrying Ligeia ('I met her first and most frequently in some large, old, decaying city near the Rhine') the narrator commits himself to Continental Romanticism; after Ligeia's demise, when he remarries Lady Rowena Trevanion of Tremaine, 'fair-haired and blue-eyed,' a girl apparently from Cornwall, narrator succumbs to the false lure of British Romanticism; in the end, however, his first and truer love reasserts her claim upon his intellectual fealty. I admit a case can be made for this. You'd be hard put to guess how convincing that case is, but if you've recently *read* Poe's 'Ligeia,' you may feel (as I do) that this theory about its 'meaning' is too clever by half.

It's incontestable, though, that Ligeia herself is associated, in Narrator's mind, with *knowledge*. She is described, admired, adored, nay, worshipped, not so much for what she looks like, or for who she is, but for *what she knows*, what contemplation of her boundless mind makes Narrator (he nowhere names himself) think that he knows. The Beloved as Wisdom-

Figure. One thing, though, which he *doesn't* know is rather surprising: 'And now, while I write, a recollection flashes upon me that I have *never known* the paternal name of her who was my friend and my betrothed, and who became the partner of my studies, and finally the wife of my bosom.' Husband, Husband, what, O what did you and your friend, your betrothed, the partner of your studies and the wife of your bosom talk about during the long hours in seminar which comprised your courtship? Did you never think to ask her her paternal name? Ah, Edgarpoe, you don't becloud *our* clear view of this romance with your obfuscations. You knew that name well, too well for remembrance. You caused yourself to pretend it was forgotten.

Deep as is his love for Ligeia, deeper still is a certain knowledge she possesses and represents to her adoring husband. Into this knowledge she seems to promise to initiate him. Nor should this surprise us, who have met Ligeia before—at least we have already met a *spirit*, if not a lady on the Rhine, who possessed that rather singular cognomen. The chief appeal of the name 'Ligeia' to Edgarpoe was, I think—I have tried to think as he thought and to hear with his ear—its chief appeal is, this is the only conceivable feminine name (assuming it to be such) which rhymes with the Great Key Word, *Idea*:

> Ligeia! Ligeia!
> 　　My beautiful one!
> Whose harshest idea
> 　　Will to melody run...
>
> Ligeia! wherever
> 　　Thy image may be,
> No magic may sever
> 　　Thy music from thee,

—as we remember from 'Al Aaraaf,' where this lady appears as the disembodied embodiment of Intellectual Beauty. In the tale, all her melodious wisdom seems to Husband to be concentrated in the expression of her eyes—

> How for long hours have I pondered upon it! What was it—that something more profound than the well of Democritus—which lay far within the pupils of my beloved? What *was* it? I was possessed with a passion to discover...
>
> 　　There is no point, among the many incomprehensible anomalies of the science of mind, more thrillingly exciting than the fact—never, I believe, noticed in the schools—that in our endeavors to recall to memory something long forgotten, we often find ourselves *upon the very verge of* remembrance, without being able, in the end, to remember...

So, it appears, the knowledge all but revealed in Ligeia's luminous eyes is *something already known but forgotten*, a not-quite-vanished memory of some primal condition, anterior to this life. 'I was sufficiently aware of her supremacy,' says Husband, 'to resign myself with a child-like confidence, to her guidance through the chaotic world of metaphysical investigation,' knowing that 'I might at length pass onward to the goal of a wisdom too divinely precious not to be forbidden.'

Already we have the clues in hand to trace the parameters of an Archetype. The Archetype of the Fall of Man. Here are the elements: a Beloved Woman, Forbidden Knowledge, an irresistible compulsion to possess the latter by possessing the former. But we must not think that Poe is going to give us a Fortunate Fall. It is already subliminally clear that the forbidden wisdom, sought here under Ligeia's all-knowing tutelage, by the process of remembering back before the beginning of one's present existence, is of the same kind as that intellectual destination toward which the mariner hurtled, half unwitting, in 'MS. Found in a Bottle': 'It is evident that we are hurrying onward to some exciting knowledge—some never-to-be-imparted secret, whose attainment is destruction.'

Ligeia's husband comes closer than did the mariner to defining that forbidden secret, since he has taken a cram course from his wife. 'I have spoken of the learning of Ligeia: it was immense. . . .' She epitomizes all knowledge, all wisdom, all learning. She is also the epitome of ideality, or spirit, a quality imparted to Husband by the haunting expression of her eyes. No merely human eyes, however lovely, ever held such mysteries, such clues to the unifying spirit which invisibly presides over the wayward chaos of our mortal world:

> And (strange, oh strangest mystery of all!) I found, in the commonest objects of the universe, a circle of analogies to that expression.

He finds analogies to the sentiment aroused within him 'by her large and luminous orbs' (a term more apt for the moon than for the eye)—analogies in a growing vine, in 'the contemplation of a moth, a butterfly, a chrysalis, a stream of running water.' 'I have felt it,' he adds, 'in the ocean—in the falling of a meteor. I have felt it in the glances of unusually aged people. And there are one or two stars in heaven. . . . I have been filled with it by certain sounds from stringed instruments, and not infrequently by passages from books. . . .'

In short, this is an anatomy of the universe, passing from the lowliest individual plant and animal lives through the life-giving element (water), into the outer spaces of the stars and meteors, thence beyond the fixities of matter into the existence of the spirit (in the 'unusually aged,' such as the crew of the spectral ship in 'MS. Found in a Bottle'), and thence still farther outward to the music of the spheres, culminating in pure thought, as recorded in 'passages from books.' What a gaze had Ligeia! *Quels yeux!*

As I think again of this progression of analogies, it looks this time as though the *same ethereal quality* pervades the living creatures, inanimate things, the heavenly bodies, man's own sensations and his thought. By further analogy all of these are interchangeable with one another, partaking of the same ideality by which they resemble Ligeia's wondrous gaze. This interpenetration of the organic and the inorganic is perceptible only to the most highly organized sensibility, felt only by the most suprasensient nervous system, one in which the reactions of the body have become infused with the motions of the soul. Ligeia, it would seem, doesn't even have to make an effort so to perceive the world around her, it is her nature to make such perceptions visible to those—to one in particular—who truly love her, and who worship the reflection of her wisdom in her eyes.

The interpenetration of organic and inorganic, of matter and spirit by each other's essence, is dramatized again in 'The Fall of the House of Usher' and proves a principle of existence itself in 'Eureka.' There we will find that matter and spirit differ not in essence but in degree; their essence is in fact the same. This abstract postulate is essential to Poe's universe; because he really believes it to be true, both the terrors and the ecstasies of his tales are necessary and not to be avoided. But such speculations, in 'Ligeia,' are merely hinted at, presented analogically, referred to a still deeper, more secret mystery which they merely reflect.

Ligeia's husband, as we have been noticing, adores her, worships her, feels unworthy of her love, stands to her as a child before its mother, as an acolyte before his priestess. In fact Ligeia is herself a condensation of several relationships familiar in Romantic literature, as also in the literature of 'Romance . . . that spirit which . . . presided, as they tell, over marriages ill-omened.' Ligeia is both her husband's Muse and Sacred Mother. Now it is clear why Husband has never dared to ask her or remind himself of her 'paternal name'; for if he did, he would have to face up to its being the same as his mother's. Nor would her married name be any better—hence we never learn *his* paternal name—since married to him, she bears the name of *his* father.

As Muse, as Mother-Figure, Ligeia resembles in several aspects that mythical abstraction come to life in a particular woman whom Robert Graves has revived yet again in our time and called The White Goddess. The algolagnic heroine is indeed a persistent visitant of literature, and in Ligeia we have Poe's fullest representation of 'La Belle Dame Sans Merci.' It is typical of Poe that her beauty is incarnate in an intellectual principal which unifies sensation and thought, matter and spirit, and—as we shall see—life and death. These are the gifts comprising her knowledge both sacred and forbidden, and intrinsic with her love at once all-giving and all-demanding. A dangerous woman to lose your heart to.

And this paragon of superhuman and metaphysical virtue is no seraph, as in 'Al Aaraaf,' but indeed a woman, 'most violently prey to the tumultuous vultures of stern passion,' a passion which her luckless husband quails to see in 'the miraculous expansion of those eyes which at once so delighted and appalled me.' Now, *vultures* (or condors), wherever met in Poe, signify, as in 'Sonnet—To Science,' our enslavement to Time in this real world where flesh is carrion. Passion, as we know from 'Al Aaraaf' and 'The Colloquy of Monos and Una,' is the affliction of an impure nature, one not sufficiently devoted to the transcendence of its own fallen state to be worthy of inhabiting the paradisal star where purer spirits dwell. And Ligeia herself is 'a prey to the tumultuous vultures of stern passion!' It begins to seem as though this Muse and Sacred Mother is also an impassioned woman, covetous of her lover's body, desirous of his being prey to an equally tumultuous passion—for her.

But Poe was impotent. We have seen the evidence. We have the diagnosis from his psychiatrist, Dr. Princess Bonaparte. Professor Krutch anticipated her findings with his more cursory examination of the patient. I have to find their findings acceptable. The problem, in the story, in which the feckless husband represents some of the fantasies of Edgar Allan Poe, is this: What can an impotent lover do when his beloved is aroused to 'the tumultuous vultures of stern passion'? A very interesting question, since he makes *her* the prey of the vultures, whereas in fact (were any of this a fact) she would make *him* the prey of her passions. Which would make *her* a vulture. Alas, what can he do?

He can solve everything by wishing her dead so hard that she dies. Apotheosized by both a 'passage from books' and a poem on her lips, the poem of her own composing. Poe, always concentrating all the resources of his prose to the production of a unified effect, had prepared for the event. Perhaps, in Ezra Pound's phrase, he had 'over-prepared the event.' A passage from a book appears as epigraph to the tale. The same passage reappears at the end of the paragraph which itemized all the things, from chrysalis to the music of the spheres, of which Husband thought while gazing in Ligeia's 'divine orbs':

> And the will therein lieth, which dieth not. Who knoweth the mysteries of the will, with its vigor? For God is but a great will pervading all things by nature of its intentness. Man doth not yield him to the angels, nor unto death utterly, save only through the weakness of his feeble will.

Quoted from Joseph Glanvill, according to Poe; though according to Edward Davidson the locus of such sentiments in Glanvill's work 'has so far escaped detection' (*Poe: A Critical Study*, p. 77). No matter whether the attribution be apocryphal or not; Glanvill, 'whom,' says Saintsbury in his history of English literature, 'the echoing magnificence of a sentence from him, prefixed to Poe's "Ligeia," may have made known to many more than have read him in his originals,' provided Poe with as much glamor as Poe bestowed on him. For by attributing the above-quoted doctrine to Glanvill, Poe associates it with the seventeenth-century scholar who upheld both the objective study of Nature (he was an early defender of the Royal Society) and the truth of witchcraft (in *Sadducismus Triumphatus*). Not only does this suggest to the reader that he may take his pick, for all it matters, between science and witchcraft, reason and belief, to account for the anthropomorphism of the passage. It suggests also that Ligeia's wisdom encompasses all of the contrarieties and antinomies suggested by Glanvill's intellectual and supernatural pursuits.

Ligeia is apotheosized by a poem—her own poem—whispered by her dying lips. Dying, she wishes most of all for life; living, she had written a poem in which the angels watch a troupe of mimes act out 'the play [that] is the tragedy, Man / And its hero, the conqueror Worm.' The Worm is Death, imagined by Ligeia as a serpent which writhes and devours men, amid

> . . . much of Madness, and more of Sin
> And Horror, the soul of the plot!

All this is done by actors emulating 'God on high' and

> Mere puppets . . . who come and go
> At the bidding of vast formless things
> That shift the scenery to and fro,
> Flapping from out their condor wings
> Invisible Woe!

The poem is a condensation of the tale, and the philosophy—if it can be called one—which it presents tells us that life is an unassuaged disaster, an unequal battle between mankind and inexorable Death, enacted for the amusement of angels who make no move on man's behalf although the horror of the show makes even these angels 'pallid and wan.' Although *this* is life, Ligeia herself would rather live than die; and dying, she affirms (for the third time in the tale) the epigraph Poe claims to have borrowed from Glanvill:

'O God!' half shrieked Ligeia, leaping to her feet and extending her arms aloft . . . 'O God! O Divine Father!—shall these things be undeviatingly so!—shall this conqueror be not once conquered? Are we not part and parcel in Thee? Who—who knoweth the mysteries of the will with its vigor? Man doth not yield him to the angels, *nor unto death utterly*, save only through the weakness of his feeble will.'

Even as she repeats again the sentence from Glanvill, 'She died.'

I must confess that Ligeia's performance as a poet casts a bit in doubt, for me, her prowess as Giantess of the Intellect. Assuming, that is, that she really is, as Husband thinks, equally gifted in all things. I mean, the author of 'The Conqueror Worm' is hardly as divine a singer as Husband thought. Her poem, to be blunt about it, is a piece of fustian, not a patch on Blake's 'O Rose, thou art sick,' a mere eight-liner which suggests far, far more than it says. 'The Conqueror Worm,' on the contrary, says right out all that it could suggest, nor do its banal rhythm or obvious imagery leave anything—*anything*—to *our* imagination. So I take Ligeia-as-Poet as putative. Anyway, the poem is really only the prelude to her last words. Glanvill's.

Those words imply that if death is but a failure of our will, then our will can triumph over death if only volition be strong enough—that is, as strong as God's. For, as Ligeia half-shrieked, 'Are we not part and parcel in Thee?' So then, if we are, why can we not *will ourselves not to die*?

Or do Ligeia's last words mean, *We can will someone else not to die.* Ligeia, as everyone knows, comes back to this life again, taking over—*quel frisson!*—the body, the very corpse, of her husband's *second wife*. When Rowena is on her deathbed she arises and totters into the center of the chamber, looking, breathing, seeming for all the world like the Lady Ligeia. Although Rowena Trevanion of Tremaine was slight and fair-haired and Ligeia had been statuesque and dark, Rowena, dying, becomes raven-haired and tall, tall as Ligeia. Is this Ligeia willing her own metempsychosis, or is it her husband wishing her back to life-in-death a second time?

But we have left Husband bereft, after her first dying. We must see what he does with his life thereafter.

He's a rich widower now, for 'Ligeia had brought me far more, very far more, than ordinarily falls to the lot of mortals.' With this wealth he purchases an old abbey in England, and although prostrate with grief he somehow finds the energy completely to redecorate the interior of this capacious structure. The language here is revealing. The exterior of the abbey and its situation are described with almost every adjective in the Gothic repertoire: wildest, least frequented, gloomy and dreary grandeur, savage aspect, melancholy and time-honored memories, utter abandonment, remote and unsocial region, verdant decay. To this diction of the decadence wrought by ruin and time is joined the diction of decadence wrought by the human will, as Husband now describes the fitting-out of the interior in 'a display of more than regal magnificence':

> Alas, I feel how much even of incipient madness might have been discovered in the gorgeous and fantastic draperies, in the solemn carvings of Egypt, in the wild cornices and furniture, in the Bedlam pattern of the carpets of tufted gold.

In the midst of all this wild opulence he 'had become a bounden slave to the trammels of opium,' and the description that follows is wilder still, as though the very architecture partook of the distorted involutions of his opium dreams. He describes the bridal chamber into which he led 'the fair-haired and blue-eyed Lady Rowena Trevanion, of Tremaine':

> . . . and here there was no system, no keeping, in the fantastic display, to take hold upon the memory. The room lay in a high turret of the castellated abbey, was pentagonal in shape, and of capacious size . . .

It is a bizarre jumble of window-glass from Venice, a ceiling carved in Semi-Gothic, Semi-Druidical devices, from which hangs a Saracen censor, flickering over the Eastern ottomans and the Indian bridal-couch 'with a pall-like canopy above.' In each of the five corners stands a huge sarcophagus, 'but in the draping of the apartment lay, alas! the chief fantasy of all': as the visitor to the apartment moved to the center of the room, 'he saw himself surrounded by an endless succession of . . . ghastly forms . . . giving a hideous and uneasy animation to the whole.'

Some readers have taken the décor in Lady Rowena's bower to represent Poe's ideal conception of the well-appointed chamber. But how different is this grotesque medley of sinister shapes, gloomy devices, and psychedelic shadows, from the tranquil bower of dreams in the Faubourg Saint Germain where we found Monsieur Dupin. No, Ligeia's successor and Husband are in a bower which externalizes the narrator's disordered mind, as does the earlier dream-chamber of Prince Mentoni in 'The Assignation,' that 'apartment whose unparalleled splendor' made the observer 'dizzy with luxuriousness' as 'the senses were oppressed by mingling and conflicting perfumes.' Mentoni's chamber anticipates the remarried husband's:

> In the architecture and embellishment . . . the evident design had been to dazzle and astound. Little attention had been paid to the decora of what is technically called *keeping*, or to the proprieties of nationality. The eye wandered from object to object, and rested on none . . .

Yet, in his 'Philosophy of Furniture,' Poe had created an ideal décor in which '*Repose* speaks in all' of the 'effects,' and where a single lamp with 'a plain crimson-tinted ground-glass shade,' hanging from the ceiling, 'throws a tranquil but magical radiance over all.' True, this chamber is, to our taste, rather opulent and it resembles in many particulars both the dream-bower of Mentoni and the bridal chamber made for Rowena. But the difference is all in the disarrangements there of the elements which are harmoniously unified in 'Philosophy of Furniture.' These disordered chambers are, like Poe's landscapes and the geography of his voyages, the projections outward into objects of the mind that both perceives and creates them.

Into such a chamber the husband now conducts his new bride. In so gloomily sinister a fashion has he furnished it that even he must ask, 'Where were the souls of the haughty family of the bride, when, through thirst of gold, they permitted to pass the threshold of an apartment *so* bedecked, a maiden and a daughter so beloved?' The room which poor Rowena has entered is at once three *loci*: her bridal bower is her death chamber, and both, as I've said, are really in the mind—indeed, they *are* the mind, of the narrator.

What a marriage. Here, in this very chamber, he says, 'I passed, with the Lady of Tremaine, the unhallowed hours of the first month of our marriage.' He notes with pleasure that his wife 'shunned me and loved me but little'; for his part, 'I loathed her with a hatred belonging more to a demon than to man.' Now he can think of nothing but—Ligeia:

> Ligeia, the beloved, the august, the entombed. I revelled in recollections of her purity, of her wisdom, of her lofty—her ethereal nature, of her passionate, her idolatrous love.

And now he tells us that he's a habitual opium-eater. 'In the excitement of my opium dreams,' he says, he calls aloud Ligeia's name, 'as if, through the wild eagerness, the solemn passion, the consuming ardor of my longings for the departed, I could restore her to the pathways she had abandoned—ah, *could* it be forever?—upon earth.'

Need we be surprised that Ligeia is soon to reappear? Or that Rowena, so injured and insulted by Husband, will soon fall sick—with *the very same wasting disease* that carried off Ligeia? Or that once taken ill, Rowena will be terrified by the illusory movements of sinister shapes swirling about her?

We are now at the point in the tale where the unbelievable is about to happen. Unbelievable, that is, if you can believe any of what has happened thus far. The fact that we stay with Poe clear to the end, that despite the pompous inflation of style and the grotesqueness of situation and event, we read him through with enough suspension of disbelief to be ready for his final *frisson*—all this bespeaks Poe's success in mastering his obsessional materials by imposing upon them a coherent and necessary literary form. We give 'Ligeia' enough credence not in spite of its stylistic grotesqueries but because of them. Poe, as we know, could write as clearly and as perspicuously as Defoe when he wanted to. But who would tolerate the plain style of Monsieur Dupin's sidekick in the mouth of Ligeia's husband? Each tells his own tale in the language, in the rhythms, in the rhetoric most appropriate to his own character. And that character is, for Poe, embodied in his mental, or as Poe calls it, his 'psychal' state. The state of mind of the narrator in 'Ligeia' is one of terrible, nearly insupportable exacerbation; he is living out compulsive fantasies which obtrude upon the opium trances in which he has sought refuge. But let's not mistake for this distraught and, I think, technically insane narrator, the mind of Edgar Poe. For it is Poe, with his equally tortured sensibility, who has exercised his intellectual and artistic faculties—has exhibited them in the fullness of their control—to make us aware of the mental disorder of his character, the husband of both Rowena and Ligeia.

Meanwhile, back in the deadroom, Rowena must die. She must recapitulate the death of Ligeia while Husband, half narcotized, looks on, helpless to save her from her death. Indeed, he may have caused, may be causing it. Does he really murder Rowena? Some critics have approached this tale with the delicacy of the Prefect of Police, and disputations among them argue such points as this, as well as whether the tale is a ghost story or a love story (whose?). Besides, does Ligeia reappear in Rowena's body because *she* wills to come back to her husband, or because her husband wills her return? Roy Basler concluded that Husband poisons Rowena and imagines the rest. Mme Bonaparte identifies everybody in the tale, as is usual with her, with real persons: Husband=Edgar; Ligeia=Elizabeth Arnold; Rowena=Virginia Clemm but also Frances Allen. Were we to take Mme Bonaparte as literally as she takes Poe, would we have any right or reason to take either of them seriously?

Let there be light. If my mythologized interpretation of Ligeia as Muse and Mother-Goddess has any merit, then it follows that Rowena is the poor mortal woman whom the adept of the Mother Goddess loves, as a substitute or surrogate for the aforesaid Divine She. Now, it is a fact that *Narrator does not describe Rowena's eyes.* He does not even mention them. She is all flesh, all flesh; no wonder he turns from her with loathing and 'a hatred belonging more to a demon than to man,' takes dope, and dreams of the unifying, tranquillizing, ethereal qualities of his lost tutelary spirit. And even Ligeia had become lost to him because, spirit though she was, she was also a mortal body, decaying, and 'a prey to the tumultuous vultures of stern passion.' Rowena resembles Ligeia only at the lower end of the spectrum of possible correspondences. Rowena rises to Ligeia-like spirituality only at the moment when she passes from life into death. Then, and only then, Ligeia's spirit passes into Rowena's body, and she looks like Ligeia. Several times, Narrator has examined her *eyelids* during her death-throes. Now, at the final moment, he at last mentions her *eyes*:

> 'Here then, at last,' I shrieked aloud, 'can I never—can I never be mis-taken—these are the full, and the black, and the wild eyes—of my lost love—of the Lady—of the LADY LIGEIA.'

Terror, terror, terror grips us the first time we read this tale. A strange numbness in the heart, a willingness to be frightened at the very moment we would dismiss the spectre as a story-teller's audacious imposition. But we don't dismiss the imposition, we give in to the sensation of being terrified as though revelling in a voluptuous excitation. Why are we unwilling or unable to see through this most horrible trick of Hoaxiepoe's? Or, if able to see through it, unable to free ourselves from illusions exposed as illusion? Is it because we are reminded of something we are on the verge of remembering but cannot?

Later, after many readings in which the tale of 'Ligeia' has never lost its power to move me, I have asked myself what is the composition of that feeling which grips me now, as ever before, when I retrace the fantastic dreams of this narrator imagined by Edgar Poe. I recognized that terror contributes but half of the power that numbs the heart and makes the hackles rise. The other half comes from pity, pity, pity.

How sore, how mortal was the wound that left the *persona* through whom Poe speaks so bereft that after his first and primal love he could know no other? So overwhelmingly is he possessed by that first love that, should *he* choose to succeed the 'raven-black' hair and brilliant black eyes of Ligeia with 'the fair-haired and blue-eyed' Rowena, it first seems to him 'a moment of mental alienation' when he betrayed his first love's memory by leading to the altar his second, so different in aspect. Then his love for her turns to hatred and loathing, a loathing and hatred he had unconsciously anticipated by decorating her bridal suite as a psychedelic torture-chamber. Whether the three drops of red liquid which fall into Rowena's wine-glass are *really* emanations from the spirit of the jealous Ligeia, or are poison placed there by the husband in his opium jag, or are his wild remembrance of the bloody sputum of the author's dying mother, Rowena must die—if indeed she ever lived savē as a wraith in the guilt-haunted imagination of Ligeia's acolyte who could love no one, love nothing, but the almost-remembered actuality of Ligeia. Whether Rowena be wraith or woman, how can she sustain her own beauty, her own features, the color of her own eyes and hair, in the imagination of a lover who is so completely imprisoned by his first, his only, his only possible devotion?

It seems impossible to doubt that the prototypes of these experiences in the tale were the death of Eddie's mother, his guilty transference of love to Mrs. Allan, then later to various childhood sweethearts and at last to poor Virginia Clemm, each of whom died in the same lingering way and seemed no doubt to Edgar to be a resurrection of her predecessors only to re-enact her predecessor's death. Poor, poor Eddie Poe. But these hapless accidents of one miserable scrivener's biography are in 'Ligeia' successfully mythologized, universalized, raised to the level of archetype. Strange though the combination seems, in Poe, of ideality with necrophilia, here he has imagined a condition of blessedness, its loss, the loser's search for its recurrence in another love-object, the intensification of that love into hatred for its substitute and longing for the lost love, and a final apotheosis in which the lost love seems to reappear.

Erotic interest is all but completely censored, is quite subsumed in Ligeia's metaphysics. Despite the one allusion to her 'stern passion,' there is no physical contact mentioned in either of Narrator's 'marriages.' This delicacy, or squeamishness, fooled several generations of readers into thinking that Poe was a spiritual writer—if they didn't take him for a fiend. Of course we can now read Poe with less prejudice, and so we recognize that it is this suppressed erotic intensity which throbs and shudders throughout the tale. When Rowena is in her dying hours, Narrator cries,

> But why shall I minutely detail the unspeakable horrors of the night? Why shall I pause to relate how, time after time, until near the period of the gray dawn, this hideous drama of revivification was repeated; how each terrific relapse was only into a sterner and apparently more irredeemable death; how each agony wore the aspect of a struggle with some invisible foe. . . . Let me hurry to a conclusion.

Are these the throes of the dying body struggling to live, or of the living body struggling to die? What other experience does this description suggest than the repeated, excited violation of the body in successive, spasmodic orgasm? Death is usually a metaphor of sexual experience, all the more so for Poe because his own nature did not permit him to know, nor did the prurient mores of his class and time allow him to describe, sexual union in a normal way. Through the psychic identity of sexual extinction with death itself, Poe is enabled imaginatively to 'possess' the beloved by experiencing the moment of her bodily dissolution.

I have already mentioned similarities between 'Ligeia' and 'The Assignation.' In that story there are other interesting analogies to this one besides the décor of the dreamer's chamber. 'The Assignation' is a tale of a consummated love—the consummation comes in the simultaneous suicides of the lordly dreamer-lover and his forbidden beloved, the Marchesa Aphrodite. Here, in this early tale, are some of the nascent images which will exfoliate in 'Ligeia.' The Marchesa, whose given name identifies her at once as indeed a Love Goddess, is, like Helen in the famous poem, and like Ligeia, described as having hyacinthine hair and hands of marble. These associations link all three beloved women with classic beauty, with the ideal purity of the ancient world, with the dignity of the earliest age of myth and epic. The Prince Mentoni achieves perpetual union with his Aphrodite by dying into her death. Ligeia's husband is not so fortunate, his beloved dies before him, and he must somehow summon her back, wish herself to will herself back, into life. But this cannot be. All that can be managed, while men suffer in their bodies and their spirits are tortured by the vultures of passion and the passage of time, is to bring her back to the instant of her leaving, as she slipped beyond the veil of the beyond. Closer than this we cannot come in this life to the mysteries of a knowledge which is forbidden to mortality, forbidden with a tabu as intense and as absolute as that which makes impossible a grown son's desire for the all-consoling love which as an infant he felt lavished on him by his mother, and which makes unthinkable his reciprocation.

Thus as fiction, as myth, as psychological archetype, the pattern of imagined action in 'Ligeia' is not only fantastic but self-consistent—and true, in its kinky way, to human experience as well as to the accidents of one particularly blighted life. Yet the myths of antiquity and the psychology of today do not fully elucidate this singular imaginative construct. For Poe, death is a metaphor of sexuality—and of something more. It is the multiple associations of death in Poe's work which lend his tales their particular fascination, their concatenation of terror and sublimity inextricably intermingled.

Death is personal extinction, the obliteration of this particular bundle of sensations and memories, and therefore terrifying. Death is also deliverance from the memories and sensations in which this particular person, this particular combination of atoms divided from the unity whence they came, is imprisoned—and thus death is welcome. Death is the necessitous apocalypse in which all divided creation hurtles toward instantaneous reunion in the oneness from which it had been sundered. Thus death, the most feared, is also the bringer of deliverance in a metapersonal ecstasy. But that is another story, as we see in the *Narrative of Arthur Gordon Pym* and in *Eureka*.

JOHN T. IRWIN

The White Shadow

That the figure at the pole is a white shadow, indeed, that it is Pym's own shadow, which he does not recognize, seems more than likely when one considers the similarities between the ending of *Pym* and the numerous examples of the trope of the white shadow in Romantic tradition (particularly among authors whom Poe admired). Thus in Coleridge's poem "Constancy to an Ideal Object" (1828), the speaker is haunted by a "yearning Thought" that "liv'st but in the brain," the thought of an idealized woman who is synonymous with home. Yet this ideal can only be realized when "Hope and Despair meet in the porch of Death!" (1:455-56). Without this companion, any place where the speaker dwells is like "a becalméd bark, / Whose Helmsman on an ocean waste and wide / Sits mute and pale his mouldering helm beside" (1:456). The poem concludes with the speaker's acknowledgment that this ideal object is an unrecognized shadow image that he himself has projected:

> And art thou nothing? Such thou art, as when
> The woodman winding westward up the glen
> At wintry dawn, where o'er the sheep track's maze
> The viewless snow-mist weaves a glist'ning haze,
> Sees full before him, gliding without tread,
> An image with a glory round its head;
> The enamoured rustic worships its fair hues,
> Nor knows he makes the shadow, he pursues!
>
> (1:456)

In James Hogg's *The Private Memoirs and Confessions of a Justified Sinner* (1824), the scenario of the white shadow in the mist is part of a classic double story—the murder of the good George Colwan by his evil half-brother, Robert Wringhim. The malicious Wringhim dogs his brother's every movement like "the shadow . . . cast from the substance, or the ray of light from the opposing denser medium." To escape Wringhim's constant shadowing, George goes for a walk at daybreak in the mist and beholds "to his astonishment, a bright halo in the cloud of haze, that rose in a semicircle over his head like a pale rainbow." He realizes that "the lovely vision" is "his own shadow on the cloud" with "a halo of glory round a point of the cloud . . . whiter and purer than the rest." Seating himself "on the pinnacle of the rocky precipice," George believes that he has finally escaped from his brother's annoying presence, unaware that Wringhim has followed him and is at that instant approaching from behind to push him off the cliff:

> The idea of his brother's dark and malevolent looks coming at that moment across his mind, he turned his eyes instinctively to the right, to the point where that unwelcome guest was wont to make his appearance. . . . What an apparition was there presented to his view! He saw, delineated in the cloud, the shoulders, arms, and features of a human being of the most dreadful aspect. The face was the face of his brother, but dilated to twenty times the natural size. Its dark eyes gleamed on him through the mist.
>
> . . . he took it for some horrid demon . . . that . . . in taking on itself the human form, had miscalculated dreadfully on the size, and presented itself thus to him in a blown-up, dilated frame of embodied air, exhaled from the caverns of death or the regions of devouring fire. He was farther confirmed in the belief that it was a malignant spirit on perceiving that it approached him across the front of a precipice, where there was not footing for thing of mortal frame.

As the apparition continues to approach, George turns to flee, but "the very first bolt that he made in his flight he came in contact with a *real* body of flesh and blood. . . . George then perceived that it was his brother; and being confounded between the shadow and the substance, he knew not what he was doing or what he had done."

Whether or not the image of George's brother is the apparition of a malignant spirit, there is certainly nothing supernatural about the white shadow in the mist. In Poe's day one of the best known examples of this phenomenon was the gigantic spectre of the Brocken in north Germany. Coleridge had climbed the Brocken on Whitsunday 1799, with a group of English students from Göttingen, but failed to see the phantom; while in 1845 De Quincey described the spectre in one of the "Suspiria de Profundis" articles in *Blackwood's*, a description based not on a real ascent of the Brocken but on an ascent "executed in dreams . . . under advanced stages in the development of opium." The best contemporary scientific account of the phenomenon was in David Brewster's *Letters on Natural Magic* (1832), a book that Poe quotes at length in his essay "Maelzel's Chess-Player" (14:7-8) published in April 1836. In his chapter on natural optical illusions, Brewster recounts two separate sightings of the spectre of the Brocken in 1797 and 1798 and explains the physical circumstances causing the appearance:

> The spectre of the Brocken and other phenomena of the same kind... are merely shadows of the observer projected on dense vapour or thin fleecy clouds, which have the power of reflecting much light. They are seen most frequently at sunrise, because it is at that time that the vapours and clouds necessary for their production are most likely to be generated; and they can be seen only when the sun is throwing his rays horizontally, because the shadow of the observer would otherwise be thrown either up in the air, or down upon the ground.... The head will be more distinct than the rest of the figure, because the rays of the sun will be more copiously reflected at a perpendicular incidence; and as from this cause the light reflected from the vapour or cloud becomes fainter farther from the shadow, the appearance of a halo round the head of the observer is frequently visible.

In *Walden* Thoreau gives us his own version of the white shadow and then cites Benvenuto Cellini's account of a similar experience as evidence of the phenomenon's relation to the angle of light and the atmospheric diffusion of moisture common in the early morning:

> As I walked on the railway causeway, I used to wonder at the halo of light around my shadow, and would fain fancy myself one of the elect.... Benvenuto Cellini tells us in his memoirs, that, after a certain terrible dream or vision which he had during his confinement in the castle of St. Angelo, a resplendent light appeared over the shadow of his head at morning and evening, ... and it was particularly conspicuous when the grass was moist with dew. This was probably the same phenomenon to which I have referred, which is especially observed in the morning, but also at other times, and even by moonlight. Though a constant one, it is not commonly noticed, and, in the case of an excitable imagination like Cellini's, it would be basis enough for superstition.

One of the places where natural optical illusions occur most frequently, as Brewster points out, is in the polar seas during temperature inversions, the kind of temperature inversion that Pym experiences when the atmosphere begins to grow warmer the closer he gets to the pole. During the final stage of the journey, Pym associates the polar region, and in particular the curtain of vapor, with extraordinary optical appearances: "Many unusual phenomena now indicated that we were entering upon a region of novelty and wonder. A high range of light gray vapour appeared constantly in the southern horizon, flaring up occasionally in lofty streaks, now darting from east to west, now from west to east, and again presenting a level and uniform summit—in short, having all the wild variations of the Aurora Borealis" (3:238). Of the two physical conditions that are required for the appearance of the white shadow, one is obviously present in the polar regions—the curtain of vapor. As to the position of the sun, Pym notes after leaving Tsalal that there was continual daylight, but as they journey farther to the south he says that the "Polar winter appeared to be coming on" and that a "sullen darkness now hovered above us" (3:240-41). The date on which Pym sees the figure in the mist, March 22, is one day after the autumnal equinox in the Southern Hemisphere. Consequently, in the South Polar region, the sun would be at the horizon for the full twenty-four hours of that day. It would be like a day-long sunrise, with half of the sun's disk always visible above the earth's edge. The sun would make a circuit of the horizon, continually throwing its rays along a horizontal plane in precisely the manner required to cast a shadow on the vapor. Further, the fact that Pym describes the shape in the mist as "a shrouded human figure" whose skin is "of the perfect whiteness of the snow" suggests that he is distinguishing between the body of the figure, the portion that would presumably be "shrouded," that is, indistinct, and its head where the whiteness of the skin would normally be exposed—a differentiation that coincides with Brewster's remark that the shadow's head with its luminous halo "will be more distinct than the rest of the figure."

In addition to the essay on natural optical illusions, Poe would have found in Brewster's work a discussion of spectral illusions that compares the physiological bases of visual, mental, and hallucinatory images—a discussion that Poe may have found especially interesting, since many of the incidents that Brewster describes involve the appearance of human figures shrouded in their grave-clothes. Brewster maintains that spectral apparitions "are nothing more than ideas or the recollected images of the mind, which in certain states of bodily indisposition have been rendered more vivid than actual impressions; or to use other words, that the pictures in the 'mind's eye' are more vivid than the pictures in the body's eye." He proposes "to show that the 'mind's eye' is actually the body's eye, and that the retina is the common tablet on which both classes of impressions are painted" as well as "all ideas recalled by the memory or created by the imagination," so that "they receive their visual existence according to the same optical laws." He continues:

> In the healthy state of the mind and body, the relative intensity of these two classes of impressions on the retina are [sic] nicely adjusted. The mental pictures are transient and comparatively feeble, and in ordinary temperaments are never capable of disturbing or effacing the direct images of visible objects. . . .
>
> In darkness and solitude, when external objects no longer interfere with the pictures of the mind, they become more vivid and distinct; and in the state between waking and sleeping, the intensity of the impressions approaches to that of visible objects. With persons of studious habits, who

are much occupied with the operations of their own minds, the mental pictures are much more distinct than in ordinary persons. . . .

According to Brewster, a hallucinatory image involves a reversal of energy that alters the relative intensities of visual images and mental images on the retina, with the result that a mental image becomes vivid enough to be taken for a visual image, indeed becomes so vivid at times as to blot out a visual image. Brewster associates a less energetic form of this reversal with that state between waking and sleep which the Romantics considered the special province of the creative imagination. As Pym's canoe approaches the curtain of vapor, he and his companions drift into a liminal state of consciousness. Pym says, "I felt a *numbness* of body and mind—a dreaminess of sensation. . . . Peters spoke little, and I knew not what to think of his apathy" (3:240-41); meanwhile the black man Nu-Nu succumbs to "drowsiness and stupor" (3:240). In Pym's case, this state lies between waking consciousness and the final sleep of the abyss. In the *Marginalia* Poe describes his own experience of drifting into the state between waking and sleep in words that have special significance for Pym's situation:

> There is . . . a class of fancies, of exquisite delicacy, which are *not* thoughts, and to which, *as yet*, I have found it absolutely impossible to adapt language. I use the word *fancies* at random, and merely because I must use *some* word; but the idea commonly attached to the term is not even remotely applicable to the shadows of shadows in question. They seem to me rather psychal than intellectual. They arise in the soul (alas, how rarely!) only at its epochs of most intense tranquillity . . . and at those mere points of time where the confines of the waking world blend with those of the world of dreams. I am aware of these "fancies" only when I am upon the very brink of sleep, with the consciousness that I am so. I have satisfied myself that this condition exists but for an inappreciable *point* of time—yet it is crowded with these "shadows of shadows"; and for absolute *thought* there is demanded time's *endurance*. (16:88)

There is obviously a connection between these "fancies," which Poe describes as "shadows of shadows," and such notions as God, spirit, and infinity, which he calls "thoughts of thought." As the fancies are *"not* thoughts" so God, spirit, and infinity are "by no means the expression of an idea, but of an effort at one." Poe says that he is aware of these fancies in that in-between state where sleeping and waking blend—"upon the very brink of sleep, with the consciousness that I am so"—a state similar to that of imagining one's own death as if it were the death of another, so that at the same time one is both dead and yet conscious that one is dead. Poe adds that he regards "the visions, even as they arise, with an awe which, in some measure, moderates or tranquilizes the ecstasy—I so regard them, through a conviction (which seems a portion of the ecstasy itself) that this ecstasy, in itself, is of a character supernal to the Human Nature—is a glimpse of the spirit's outer world; and I arrive at this conclusion—if this term is at all applicable to instantaneous intuition—by a perception that the delight experienced has, as its element, but *the absoluteness of novelty*" (16:89). One recalls in this regard Pym's characterization of the polar sea as "a region of novelty and wonder."

The visions to which Poe testifies in the *Marginalia* are clearly not external visual images, but rather something arising from within his own mind at the edge of waking consciousness, something that, because of its absolute novelty (its being beyond words), he describes as "supernal to Human Nature . . . a glimpse of the spirit's outer world." Yet the words he uses to describe his reaction to these fancies—"a conviction (which seems a portion of the ecstasy itself)," "instantaneous intuition"—make one wonder whether these "visions" have any distinct visual component at all, whether they are not rather a matter of indefinite feeling or mood, an immediate intuition of the will as motion/emotion, whose most accurate representation is music and in relation to which visual images and words must always seem unsatisfactory. At any rate, Poe says that "so entire is my faith in the *power of words*, that, at times, I have believed it possible to embody even the eva-nescence of fancies such as I have attempted to describe" (16:89):

> I have proceeded so far . . . as to prevent the lapse from *the point* of which I speak—the point of blending between wakefulness and sleep—as to prevent at will, I say, the lapse from this border-ground into the do-minion of sleep. Not that I can *continue* the condition—not that I can render the point more than a point—but that I can startle myself from the point into wakefulness—*and thus transfer the point itself into the realm of Memory*—convey its impressions, or more properly their recollections, to a situation where (although still for a very brief period) I can survey them with the eye of analysis.
>
> . . . nothing can be more certain than that even a partial record of the impressions would startle the universal intellect of mankind, by the *supremeness of the novelty* of the material employed, and of its consequent suggestions. In a word—should I ever write a paper on this topic, the world will be compelled to acknowledge that, at last, I have done an original thing. (16:90)

The main problem that these fancies present is their evanescence: they supplant one another so quickly that they never achieve the level of persistence required for the definiteness of an image. Although Poe says that he can transfer the point between waking and sleeping into the realm of memory, he seems to be able to bring into waking consciousness not the impressions themselves, but only some attenuated "recollections," perhaps memories of his own emotional response to the fleeting impressions. The fancies cannot be anything as simple as dream images, since it would be no "original thing" to embody such images in words. The extreme temporal mobility of the fancies would again suggest something musical rather than visual, or perhaps some blending of the two that reflects the "blending between wakefulness and sleep," some visual music. As Pym nears the curtain of mist, he says, "At intervals there were visible in it wide, yawning, but momentary rents, and from out these rents, within which was a chaos of flitting and indistinct images, there came rushing and mighty, but soundless winds, tearing up the enkindled ocean in their course" (3:241-42). This vision combines a glimpse of "flitting and indistinct images" with a traditional image of natural audibility (a rushing wind) and thus of natural musicality (as in the trope of the Aeolian harp), but with the musical component rendered "soundless" and thus visually represented by the fleeting indistinctness of the images. Elsewhere in the *Marginalia* Poe remarks: "I *know* that indefinitiveness is an element of the true music—I mean of the true musical expression. Give to it any undue decision—imbue it with any very determinate tone— and you deprive it, at once, of its ethereal, its ideal, its intrinsic and essential character. You dispel its luxury of dream. You dissolve the atmosphere of the mystic on which it floats" (16:29).

Whatever the status of Poe's "fancies," one thing is clear: his desire to make a fully conscious incursion into the unconscious realm of sleep and return with a written record of his impressions—that "paper" which would compel the world to acknowledge that he had "done an original thing"— parallels the desire to journey into the abyss of origin and return to the world of consciousness with some original word about the unconscious realm of death. Indeed, one might speculate that the latter is a projection of the former and that the notion of the survival of images in the unconscious state of death is derived from those images that we see in the unconscious state of sleep. It is worth recalling in this regard the traditional link between the hieroglyphics and dream interpretation, a connection that Bishop Warburton summarizes in *The Divine Legation of Moses Demonstrated:*

> The *Egyptian priests*, the first interpreters of dreams, took their rules for this species of DIVINATION, from their *symbolic* riddling, in which they were so deeply read: a ground of interpretation which would give the strongest credit to the art; and equally satisfy the diviner and the consulter: for by this time it was generally believed that their gods had given them *hieroglyphic writing*. So that nothing was more natural than to imagine that these gods, who in their opinion gave *dreams* likewise, had employed the same mode of expression in both revelations. This, I suppose, was the true original of *oneirocritic*, or the interpretation of those dreams called allegorical; that is, of dreams in general. . . . the *oneirocritics* borrowed their art of deciphering from symbolic hieroglyphics.

In *A Week on the Concord and Merrimack Rivers* (1849), Thoreau remarks that "In the mythus a superhuman intelligence uses the unconscious thoughts and dreams of men as its hieroglyphics to address men unborn." The notion that dream images are a pictographic script to be deciphered like hieroglyphics was the opinion of the preeminent modern interpreter of dreams as well. Freud writes: "If we reflect that the means of representation in dreams are principally visual images and not words, we shall see that it is even more appropriate to compare dreams with a system of writing than a language. In fact the interpretation of dreams is completely analogous to the decipherment of an ancient pictographic script such as Egyptian hieroglyphs. . . . The ambiguity of various elements of dreams finds a parallel in these ancient systems of writing" (13:177).

Now whether one interprets the gigantic shape that Pym sees in the mist as a natural optical illusion (a white shadow) or a spectral illusion (a mental image that, by a reversal of intensity in a liminal state, appears to have the independent status of a visual image), the figure displays in either case a shadowy character in the sense of being unrecognizedly self-projected. It exhibits the uncertainty of the boundary between observer and phenomenon, that condition of indeterminacy in which the observer in part creates the phenomenon he observes and thus ends by observing his own presence in a kind of veiled narcissism. Yet the characteristic human response to any disembodied self-animating image, whether natural phenomenon or spectral illusion, is to consider it as some form of spiritual appearance, some visible evidence of the unseen world. Thus, for example, Wordsworth, in his own version of the giant shadow in the mist from book 8 of *The Prelude*, describes his reaction to the extraordinary appearance of a shepherd remembered from his boyhood:

> When up the lonely brooks on rainy days
> Angling I went, or trod the trackless hills
> By mists bewildered, suddenly mine eyes
> Have glanced upon him distant a few steps,
> In size a giant, stalking through thick fog,
> His sheep like Greenland bears; or, as he stepped
> Beyond the boundary line of some hill-shadow,
> His form hath flashed upon me, glorified
> By the deep radiance of the setting sun:
> Or him have I descried in distant sky,
> A solitary object and sublime,
> Above all height! like an aerial cross
> Stationed alone upon a spiry rock
> Of the Chartreuse, for worship.

Wordsworth says that the shepherd seemed to be a creature "spiritual almost / As those of books, but more exalted far; / Far more of an imaginative form /

Than the gay Corin of the groves, who lives / For his own fancies." The direction of the passage is clear: from an extraordinary natural phenomenon (the shepherd's gigantic shadow in the mist), Wordsworth moves toward an apotheosis of the human form, first "glorified" by the sun and then transformed, through its association with the "aerial cross," into an image of that divine Good Shepherd who is the archetype of all pastoral care. When Wordsworth speaks of the shepherd as "an imaginative form," "spiritual almost as those of books," he implicitly acknowledges that in this passage he has been engaged in reading the book of nature, in making what is all too plainly a personal interpretation of the script of natural forms whereby the literal becomes the spiritual. He anticipates this objection in the remarkably defensive passage that follows the description of the shepherd:

> Call ye these appearances—
> Which I beheld of shepherds in my youth,
> This sanctity of Nature given to man—
> A shadow, a delusion, ye who pore
> On the dead letter, miss the spirit of things;
> Whose truth is not a motion or a shape
> Instinct with vital functions, but a block
> Or waxen image which yourselves have made,
> And ye adore! But blessed be the God
> Of Nature and of Man that this was so;
> That men before my inexperienced eyes
> Did first present themselves thus purified,
> Removed, and to a distance that was fit.

Wordsworth applies to the book of nature that revisionary, New Testament principle of interpreting scripture which Paul enunciates in 2 Corinthians. Comparing individual Christians to "the epistle of Christ . . . written not with ink, but with the Spirit of the living God; not in tables of stone, but in fleshy tables of the heart," Paul says that he is a minister of this "new testament; not of the letter, but of the spirit: for the letter killeth, but the spirit giveth life" (3:3-6). And he adds, "But if the ministration of death, written and engraven in stones, was glorious, so that the children of Israel could not steadfastly behold the face of Moses for the glory of his countenance; which was to be done away: How shall not the ministration of the spirit be rather glorious?" (3:7-8). Paul says that the Jews' "minds were blinded: for until this day remaineth the same vail untaken away in the reading of the old testament; which vail is done away with in Christ. . . . But we all, with open face beholding as in a glass the glory of the Lord, are changed into the same image from glory to glory, even as by the Spirit of the Lord" (3:14, 18).

For both Wordsworth and Paul, man's being is inscribed. It is a writing that can be read according to either the dead letter or the living spirit, a figure that can be interpreted either as the dark shadow of the mortal body (an inanimate "block / Or waxen image," the "ministration of death, written and engraven in stones") or as a bright reflection in a glass ("the glory of the Lord," a shining image that reverses the usual relationship between the body and its mirror double in that the beholder becomes a reflection of the image). (The word "glory," besides its general meaning of "radiance" or "splendor," has as well the specific meaning of "halo." What occurs at Christ's transfiguration, when the splendor of divinity shining through his body makes his face radiant as the sun and his garments white as snow, is known in theology as "the clarity of glory.") Clearly, the opposition of dead letter and living spirit in both Paul and Wordsworth is an image governed by the moralized black/white opposition of writing. The letter is dead because it is dark, the lithic shadow of an inanimate literality, like the engraving on a tombstone; while the meaning that must be interpreted or translated from the dark script, the quickening sense that hovers about the writing like the white page about the black outline of the characters or the nimbus about the body, is the radiant spirit.

That the figure that Pym sees in the mist is a white shadow, his own shadow unrecognized, seems especially likely when we consider the figure's association with Christ's transfiguration and resurrection, and the fact that the only narrated instance of Pym's seeing his own image in a mirror occurs during a mock resurrection in which he purposely transfigures his appearance. After the mutiny on the *Grampus*, Pym and his friends, seeking some means to overcome the numerical superiority of the mutineers and regain control of the ship, hit on the idea of dressing Pym in the clothes of a dead seaman named Hartman Rogers, who was apparently poisoned by the leader of the mutiny. Disguised as the resurrected corpse, Pym is to enter the dimly lit cabin where the mutineers have been drinking, and in the resulting confusion his friends are to overpower them. Peters adds the finishing touches to Pym's transfiguration by rubbing Pym's face "with white chalk, and afterward splotching it with blood" from a cut in his finger (3:87). The fact that Pym's face is powdered a ghostly white by his shadow self Peters points to the subsequent reversal in which Pym's dark shadow becomes the misty figure whose skin is "of the perfect whiteness of the snow." Disguised as the dead man, Pym chances to see his reflection in the cabin mirror: "I was so impressed with a sense of vague awe at my appearance and at the recollection of the terrific reality which I was thus representing, that I was seized with a violent tremour, and could scarcely summon resolution to go on with my part" (3:88). Pym's disguise is so successful that his unexpected appearance in the midst of the mutineers literally frightens their leader to death. And if the crew could mistake Pym's transfigured body for "a visitant from the world of shadows" (3:92), it is not surprising that Pym could later mistake his own transfigured shadow in the mist for a real body.

Pym notes that "the intense effect" caused by a "sudden apparition" is often due "to a kind of anticipative horror, lest the apparition *might possibly be* real" rather "than to an unwavering belief in its reality" (3:92)—a remark that is more an oblique comment on Pym's anticipatory losses of consciousness (and on the relationship of these symbolic deaths to his playing the role of a resurrected corpse) than a description of the mutineers' reaction to his appearance. Indeed, he says that "in the minds of the mutineers there was not even the shadow of a basis upon which to rest a doubt that the apparition of Rogers was indeed a revivification of his disgusting corpse, or at least its spiritual image" (3:92). Although Pym suggests that for the mutineers this apparition has removed any uncertainty about personal survival after death, his own words recast the shadow of doubt at the very moment that they claim to dispel it. The mutineers were sure, he says, that the apparition was *either* a revivified corpse *or* its spiritual image. Yet it is precisely the uncertainty between these two alternatives that is at issue. The notion of resurrection or revivification depends upon the idea of a soul that can exist independently of the body, so as to reanimate the corpse at some later time; but the mutineers' uncertainty as to whether the apparition is a body or an image points up man's inability to conceive of the soul independently of the body, his inability to imagine the soul as anything but a self-animating, disembodied image of the body. The emptiness of any notion of the soul apart from the body—the basic uncertainty of survival—is further emphasized by the fact that what the mutineers see is, as we know, neither a revivified corpse nor a spiritual image but a disguised living body, a hoax.

Pym's mock resurrection evokes as well the necessary link between the concept of resurrection and the reversal of values inherent in a black/white revenge morality. Within Christian tradition the general resurrection is synonymous with the last judgment. Body and soul are reunited as part of the definitive separation of good and evil. That separation is the ultimate revenge, a repetition and reversal of the wordly order: "So the last shall be first and the first last" (Matthew 20:16). But this bringing low of the mighty is also understood to be a destruction; it is the absolute separation of the wicked from the source of spiritual life, "the second death," as the Bible says. It is not, however, an annihilation of the wicked. After this second death their souls survive in hell, condemned to eternal punishments in which, according to Dante, the evildoer is made to passively endure what he had actively dealt out during life. Clearly, Pym's mock resurrection is part of a revenge scenario in which the good destroy the wicked and restore the order of rank that the mutineers had overturned. The fact that the leader of the mutiny is frightened to death by the "apparition" of the seaman he murdered is indicative of the precise balance of this reversal.

One of the major difficulties posed by the Christian concept of the last judgment as a final revenge is that since revenge necessarily involves repetition and reversal, any retribution that allows the wicked to remain in self-conscious existence in order to suffer eternal punishment seems incompatible with absolute finality, with the permanent arresting of repetition. That is, if the taking of revenge is an affront that imprints the desire for revenge upon the person who suffers it, an act that leaves a scar on the memory demanding its own repetition and reversal in turn, then the only revenge that would not beget this desire is one in which the victim's memory was obliterated. But such an annihilation of mnemic continuity is precisely what the last judgment does not involve; and since the wicked do not forget the affront of that "final" revenge, it must be assumed that, being wicked, neither do they forgive it. Yet if the finality of revenge at the last judgment is not constituted by an obliteration of the victim's memory, then perhaps it is achieved by an obliteration of the victim's will. The obvious objection to this is that the notion of a personal self without a will is as inconceivable as the notion of a personal self without a memory. Further, since the wicked are to suffer eternally, and since action and passion are modes of the will, personal suffering is equally inconceivable without a will.

The alternative, then, is to suppose that the revenge meted out at the last judgment leaves the evildoer's memory and will intact, thirsting for some future revenge of his own but forever prevented from carrying it out by the power of God. But again, conceptual difficulties arise; for if, according to Christian doctrine, willing evil is as much an offense against God as doing evil, then the damned soul with memory and will intact can continue to resist God's will, refusing to acknowledge His right to mastery and thus achieving a triumph of the individual will in its own personal mastery. Such resistance would transvalue the punishment and amount to a revenge of creature on Creator. This impulse to resist God's mastery as long as the individual will and memory exist is the essence of Milton's Satan, and, closer to home, of Melville's Ahab addressing the "clear spirit" whose "right worship is defiance": "I own thy speechless, placeless power; but to the last gasp of my earthquake life will dispute its unconditional, unintegral mastery in me. In the midst of the personified impersonal, a personality stands here. . . . Light though thou be, thou leapest out of darkness; but I am darkness leaping out of light, leaping out of thee!" This determination to remain the master of one's own will no matter what external force is applied or punishment inflicted (so long as that force leaves the self in existence), this impulse of the will to be a rule unto itself, to be its own God, is what it means to be wicked, to be in Satanic rebellion against the divine will. The orthodox Christian position, which holds that after the last judgment the wicked have no desire for revenge because they see and acknowledge the perfect justice of God's action, simply empties wickedness of any meaning. It is precisely because the wicked acknowledge the authority of no one's will but their own, because they refuse to admit that anyone has the right to judge of their actions, that they are punished. The contradictory impulse underlying the last judgment is to have the souls of the wicked be both dead and alive at once—alive enough to experience the suffering of punishment but dead enough not to experience the joy of willed defiance.

Every attempt to understand the finality of revenge at the last judgment leads in the same direction—to words emptied of significance, to words whose apparent meanings are found upon closer examination to be inconceivable. But perhaps this absence of significance is itself the meaning insofar as it indicates that the afterlife is without significance because it is without signs. Paul says that here "we see through a glass darkly" but there "face to face" (I Corinthians 13:12); here we know by means of signs and symbols, but there signs and symbols have ceased to exist. The difficulty is that human consciousness is itself the dark glass, the self being at once the image reflected in the mirror and the mirror of self-reflection, and that to speak of the self's survival in a realm devoid of signs and images makes no sense. The orthodox believer's reply would be that it is senseless for the finite human intellect to make itself the measure of the infinite, to make the limits of human self-consciousness the rule for conceiving of a realm wholly beyond those limits. A valid enough argument, were it not precisely a question of the persistence of *human* self-consciousness within the realm of the imageless; for although the limitations of the self cannot be made the measure of what lies beyond those limits, they remain the rule for the self's own existence, for any mnemic continuity after death. As a symbolic entity the self could not exist in an asymbolic realm.

One might argue that the notion of the self as a linguistic entity whose persistence depends on a stable mnemic inscription like the writing in a book is simply foreign to the Biblical sense of personal identity, except for the fact that this is one of the commonest Biblical images of the self, particularly in passages dealing with divine judgment and personal survival. Thus, for example, in Revelations 20:

> 12 And I saw the dead, small and great, stand before God; and the books were opened: and another book was opened, which is the book of life: and the dead were judged out of those things which were written in the books, according to their works.

13 And the sea gave up the dead which were in it; and death and hell delivered up the dead which were in them: and they were judged every man according to their works.

14 And death and hell were cast into the lake of fire. This is the second death.

15 And whosoever was not found written in the book of life was cast into the lake of fire.

The mnemic continuity of the self in this world, its personal history, is represented by one set of books in which are recorded the self's good and bad deeds—account books for the great settling of scores at the last judgment—while the mnemic continuity of the self in the next world is represented by the book of life in which one's name is inscribed if, in the accounting, the good deeds outweigh the bad. The image of the "book of life" or the "book of the living" runs through both the Old and New Testaments. In Malachi 3:16 it is called "a book of remembrance" for the Lord, a designation that indicates its doubly mnemic character; for the survival of the individual's ability to remember his personal history and connect those memories with the image of his body and his name depends upon God's preserving of the individual's name, image, and history in His own memory, the ground of all being.

It is in light of *Pym*'s juxtaposition of the kind of written survival possible for an author with the personal survival promised by Christianity that we can understand the full meaning of Poe's speculation on the origin and end of the universe in *Eureka*. In his prefatory remarks, Poe describes the life of *Eureka* after its author's death in terms of the resurrection of the body, corpus substituting for corpse:

To the few who love me and whom I love—to those who feel rather than to those who think—to the dreamers and those who put faith in dreams as in the only realities—I offer this Book of Truths, not in its character of Truth-Teller, but for the Beauty that abounds in its Truth; constituting it true. To these I present the composition as an Art-Product alone:—let us say as a Romance; or, if I be not urging too lofty a claim, as a Poem.

What I here propound is true:—therefore it cannot die:—or if by any means it be now trodden down so that it die, it will "rise again to the Life Everlasting."

Nevertheless it is as a Poem only that I wish this work to be judged after I am dead. (16:183)

If, in this scenario, the first death is that of the writing self Poe, then the second death would be that of the written self *Eureka*, a death that would result from an unfavorable judgment of the work by readers such that the book and its author would be forgotten. Poe seeks to ensure the resurrection of the body of his work, its survival in the collective human memory, by indicating the terms on which it should be judged—not as the logical truth of external reality but as the aesthetic truth of the internal reality of the imagination, that "tendency of the human intellect" in its moments of highest aspiration (as exhibited in pre-Socratic cosmologies, in Plato's *Timaeus*, in the Book of Genesis, and in numerous other myths of origin) to project itself into the void prior to its birth and after its death. Such cosmologies, though they may not be true in terms of empirical science, represent a deeper truth, for they exhibit the fundamental character of cosmology as an imposition of human structures upon a material universe indifferent to meaning. All cosmologies, from the pre-Socratic to the post-Newtonian, anthropomorphize, aestheticize, the material universe. In one basic sense, then, a modern scientific cosmology is as alogical as an aesthetic cosmology like *Eureka*, in that it aspires to describe a primal event, prior to the existence of man and the universe, as if there were a human bystander watching the event take place, though at that point there existed no place for the event to take nor any place for the bystander to stand. In relation to such an event the notion of human observation is meaningless. Yet the alogical impulse to know of an ultimate origin cannot be dismissed as merely illogical, as simply a flaw in the process of reasoning, as if there existed either a logical mode for such knowledge or the alternative of abandoning the quest. The impulse of human consciousness to transcend itself, to attain that knowledge which dissolves both the knower and the concept of "knowing," is not some accidental, dispensable aspect of self-consciousness but is fundamentally constitutive of it. Thus when Poe subtly exhibits the logical emptiness of the Christian notion of spiritual survival in *Pym*, he does so not because he feels that this demonstration frees us from the desire to know of an ultimate human destiny beyond death or because he has some more logical theory to propose in its place. The myth of the self's origin as an act of hieroglyphic doubling is just as alogical, in its pretension to know the undifferentiated and in its inability to conceive of the transition from the unselfconscious to the self-conscious, as in the Christian notion of personal survival. In using an alogical myth of the self's origin to put in question an alogical notion of the self's survival, Poe directs our attention to the problematic quality of all self-conscious existence, the fundamentally alogical status of the self.

Acknowledging the inherent contradictoriness of man's attempt to represent the origin of the universe in a linguistic discourse, Poe offers *Eureka* to "those who feel rather than to those who think." This split between thought and feeling, mind and body, which the preface of *Eureka* associates with the constitutive opposition between writing self and written self, is, in its ultimately unanalyzable, irreducible character, a microcosm of that opposition between sameness and difference, unity and multiplicity, simplicity and complexity that Poe in his cosmology attempts (unsuccessfully) to reduce to a primal Oneness, the origin and the ultimate destiny of the universe. What the poem *Eureka*, at once pre-Socratic and post-Newtonian, asserts is the truth of the feeling, the bodily intuition, that the diverse objects which the mind discovers in contemplating external nature form a unity, that they are all parts of one body which, if not infinite, is so gigantic as to be beyond both the spatial and temporal limits of human perception. In *Eureka*, then, Poe presents us with the paradox of a "unified" macrocosmic body that is without a totalizing image—an alogical, intuitive belief whose "truth" rests upon Poe's sense that cosmologies and myths of origin are forms of internal geography that, under the guise of mapping the physical universe, map the universe of desire. Like the other writers of the American Renaissance, Poe finds himself in the uncertain region between knowledge and belief, waking and dreams, between what compels him intellectually and what moves him emotionally; and like his contemporaries Poe has begun, in the very act of asserting his beliefs, to subordinate those beliefs in crucial and irrevocable ways to his knowledge by allowing that knowledge to dictate the discursive form and logical status of his assertion.

SHOSHANA FELMAN

On Reading Poetry:
Reflections on the Limits
and Possibilities
of Psychoanalytical Approaches

To account for poetry in psychoanalytical terms has traditionally meant to analyze poetry as a symptom of a particular poet. I would here like to reverse this approach, and to analyze a particular poet as a symptom of poetry.

No poet, perhaps, has been as highly acclaimed and, at the same time, as violently disclaimed as Edgar Allan Poe. The most controversial figure on the American literary scene, "perhaps the most thoroughly misunderstood of all American writers," "a stumbling block for the judicial critic," Edgar Allan Poe has had the peculiar fortune of being at once the most admired and the most decried of American poets. In the history of literary criticism, no other poet has engendered as much disagreement and as many critical contradictions. It is my contention that this critical disagreement is itself symptomatic of a *poetic effect,* and that the critical contradictions to which Poe's poetry has given rise are themselves indirectly significant of the nature of poetry.

THE POE-ETIC EFFECT: A LITERARY CASE HISTORY

No other poet has been so often referred to as a "genius," in a sort of common consensus shared even by his detractors. Joseph Wood Krutch, whose study of Poe tends to belittle Poe's stature and to disparage the value of

From *The Literary Freud: Mechanisms of Defense and the Poetic Will.* Copyright © 1980 by Shoshana Felman. Yale University Press, 1980.

his artistic achievement, nevertheless entitles his monograph *Edgar Allan Poe: A Study in Genius.* So do many other critics, who acknowledge and assert Poe's "genius" in the very titles of their essays, and thus propose to study "The Genius of Poe" (J.M.S. Robertson), *Le Génie d'Edgar Poe* (Camille Mauclair, Paris, 1925), *Edgar Allan Poe: His Genius and His Character* (John Dillon, New York, 1911), *The Genius and Character of Edgar Allan Poe* (John R. Thompson, privately printed, 1929), *Genius and Disaster: Studies in Drugs and Genius* (Jeannet A. Marks, New York, 1925), "Affidavits of Genius: French Essays on Poe" (Jean A. Alexander). "It happens to us but few times in our lives," writes Thomas W. Higginson, "to come consciously into the presence of that extraordinary miracle we call genius. Among the many literary persons whom I have happened to meet, . . . there are not half a dozen who have left an irresistible sense of this rare quality; and among these few, Poe." For Constance M. Rourke, "Poe has become a symbol for the type of genius which rises clear from its time;" The English poet A. Charles Swinburne speaks of "the special quality of [Poe's] strong and delicate genius;" the French poet Mallarmé describes his translations of Poe as "a monument to the genius who . . . exercised his influence in our country;" and the American poet James Russell Lowell, one of Poe's harshest critics, who, in his notorious versified verdict, judged Poe's poetry to include "two fifths sheer fudge," nonetheless asserts: "Mr. Poe has that indescribable something which men have agreed to call *genius*. . . . Let talent writhe and contort itself as it may, it has no such magnetism. Larger of bone and sinew it may be, but the wings are wanting."

However suspicious and unromantic the critical reader might wish to be with respect to "that indescribable something which men have agreed to call genius," it is clear that Poe's poetry produces, in a uniquely striking and undeniable manner, what might be called a *genius-effect:* the impression of some undefinable but compelling *force* to which the reader is subjected. To describe "this power, *which is felt,*" as one reader puts it, Lowell speaks of "magnetism"; other critics speak of "magic." "Poe," writes Bernard Shaw, "constantly and inevitably *produced magic* where his greatest contemporaries produced only beauty." T.S. Eliot quite reluctantly agrees: "Poe had, to an exceptional degree, the feeling for the incantatory element in poetry, of that which may, in the most nearly literal sense, be called 'the *magic* of verse.'"

Poe's "magic" is thus ascribed to the ingenuity of his versification, to his exceptional technical virtuosity. And yet, the word *magic,* "in the most nearly literal sense," means much more than just the intellectual acknowledgment of an outstanding technical skill; it connotes the effective action of something which exceeds both the understanding and the control of the person who is subjected to it; it connotes a force to which the reader has no choice but to submit. "No one could tell us what it is," writes Lowell, still in reference to Poe's genius, "and yet there is none who is not *inevitably aware* of . . . its power." "Poe," said Bernard Shaw, *"inevitably* produced magic." There is something about Poe's poetry which, like fate, is experienced as *inevitable*, unavoidable (and not just as irresistible). What is more, once this poetry is read, its inevitability is there to stay; it becomes lastingly inevitable: "it will *stick to the memory* of every one who reads it," writes P. Pendleton Cooke. And T.S. Eliot: "Poe is the author of a few . . . short poems . . which do somehow *stick in the memory.*"

This is why Poe's poetry can be defined, and indeed has been, as a poetry of *influence* par excellence, in the sense emphasized by Harold Bloom: "to inflow" = to have power over another. The case of Poe in literary history could in fact be accounted for as one of the most extreme and most complex cases of "the anxiety of influence," of the anxiety unwittingly provoked by the "influence" irresistibly emanating from this poetry. What is unique, how-ever, about Poe's influence, as about the "magic" of his verse, is the extent to which its action is unaccountably insidious, exceeding the control, the will, and the awareness of those who are subjected to it. "Poe's influence," writes T.S. Eliot, "is . . . puzzling":

> In France the influence of his poetry and of his poetic theories has been immense. In England and America it seems almost negligible. . . . And yet one cannot be sure that one's own writing has *not* been influenced by Poe.

Studying Poe's influence on Baudelaire, Mallarmé, and Valéry, Eliot goes on to comment:

> Here are three literary generations, representing almost exactly a century of French poetry. Of course, these are poets very different from each other. . . . But I think we can trace the development and descent of one particular theory of the nature of poetry through these three poets and it is a theory which takes its origin in the theory . . . of Edgar Poe. And the impression we get of the influence of Poe is the more impressive, because of the fact that Mallarmé, and Valéry in turn, did not merely derive from Poe through Baudelaire: each of them subjected himself to that influence directly, and has left convincing evidence of the value which he attached to the theory and practice of Poe himself. . . .
> I find that by trying to look at Poe through the eyes of Baudelaire, Mallarmé and Valéry, I become more thoroughly convinced of his im-portance, of the importance of his *work* as a whole. [Eliot's italics]

Curiously enough, while Poe's worldwide importance and effective influence is beyond question, critics nonetheless continue to protest and to proclaim, as loudly as they can, that Poe is unimportant, that Poe is *not* a major poet. In an essay entitled "Vulgarity in Literature" (1931) and taxing Poe with "vulgarity," Aldous Huxley argues:

> Was Edgar Allan Poe a major poet? It would surely never occur to any

English-speaking critic to say so. And yet, in France, from 1850 till the present time, the best poets of each generation—yes, and the best critics, too; for, like most excellent poets, Baudelaire, Mallarmé, Paul Valéry are also admirable critics—have gone out of their way to praise him. . . . We who are speakers of English . . . , we can only say, with all due respect, that Baudelaire, Mallarmé, and Valéry were wrong and that *Poe is not one of our major poets.*

Poe's detractors seem to be unaware, however, of the paradox that underlies their enterprise: it is by no means clear why anyone should take the trouble to write—at length—about a writer of no importance. Poe's most systematic denouncer, Yvor Winters, thus writes:

The menace lies not, primarily, in his impressionistic admirers among literary people of whom he still has some, even in England and in America, where a familiarity with his language ought to render his crudity obvious, for these individuals in the main do not make themselves permanently very effective; *it lies rather in the impressive body of scholarship.* . . . When a writer is supported by a sufficient body of such scholarship, a very little philosophical elucidation will suffice to establish him in the scholarly world as a writer whose greatness is self-evident.

The irony which here escapes the author is that, in writing his attack on Poe, what the attacker is in fact doing is adding still another study to the bulk of "the impressive body of scholarship" in which, in his own terms, "the menace lies"; so that, paradoxically enough, through Yvor Winters' study, "the menace"—that is, the possibility of taking Poe's "greatness as a writer" as "self-evident"—will indeed increase. I shall here precisely argue that, regardless of the value-judgment it may pass on Poe, this impressive bulk of Poe scholarship, the very quantity of the critical literature to which Poe's poetry has given rise, is itself an indication of its effective poetic power, of the strength with which it drives the reader to an *action*, compels him to a *reading-act.* The elaborate written denials of Poe's value, the loud and lengthy negations of his importance, are therefore very like psychoanalytical negations. It is clear that if Poe's text in effect were unimportant, it would not seem so important to proclaim, argue, and prove that he is unimportant. The fact that it so much *matters* to proclaim that Poe *does not matter* is but evidence of the extent to which Poe's poetry is, in effect, a *poetry that matters.*

Poe might thus be said to have a *literary case history,* most revealing in that it incarnates, in its controversial forms, the paradoxical nature of a strong *poetic effect*: the very poetry which, more than any other, is experienced as *irresistible* has also proved to be, in literary history, the poetry most *resisted,* the one that, more than any other, has provoked resistances.

This apparent contradiction, which makes of Poe's poetry a unique case in literary history, clearly partakes of the paradoxical nature of an *analytical effect*. The enigma it presents us with is the enigma of "the analytical" par excellence, as stated by Poe himself, whose amazing intuitions of the nature of what he calls "analysis" are strikingly similar to the later findings of psychoanalysis:

> The mental features discoursed of as the analytical are, in themselves, but little susceptible of analysis. *We appreciate them only in their effects.*

Because of the very nature of its strong "effects," of the reading-*acts* that it provokes, Poe's text (and not just Poe's biography or his personal neurosis) is clearly an analytical case in the history of literary criticism, a case that suggests something crucial to understand in psychoanalytic terms. It is therefore not surprising that Poe, more than any other poet, has been repeatedly singled out for psychoanalytical research, has persistently attracted the attention of psychoanalytic critics.

THE PSYCHOANALYTICAL APPROACHES

The best known and most influential psychoanalytic studies of Poe are the 1926 study by Joseph Wood Krutch, *Edgar Allan Poe: A Study in Genius*, and the 1933 study by Marie Bonaparte, *Edgar Poe: Étude psychanalytique*, later to appear in English as the *Life and Works of Edgar Allan Poe*. More recently, Jacques Lacan has published a more limited study of one tale by Poe, "The Seminar on *The Purloined Letter*," first published in 1966.

Joseph Wood Krutch:
Ideological psychology, or the approach of normative evaluation

For Joseph Wood Krutch, Poe's text is nothing other than an accurate transcription of a severe neurosis, a neurosis whose importance and significance for "healthy" people is admittedly unclear in Krutch's mind. Poe's "position as the first of the great neurotics has never been questioned," writes Krutch ambiguously. And less ambiguously, in reply to some admiring French definitions of that position: "Poe 'first inaugurated the poetic conscience' only if there is no true poetry except the poetry of morbid sensibility." "He must stand or fall with that whole body of neurotic literature of which his works furnish the earliest complete example." Since Poe's works, according to Krutch, "bear no conceivable relation . . . to the life of any people, and it is impossible to account for them on the basis of any social or intellectual tendencies or as the expression of the spirit of any age," the only possible approach is a biographical one, and "any true understanding" of the work is contingent upon a diagnosis of Poe's nervous malady. Krutch thus diagnoses in Poe a pathological condition of sexual impotence, the result of a "fixation" on his mother, and explains Poe's literary drive as a desire to compensate for, on the one hand, the loss of social position of which his foster father had deprived him, through the acquisition of literary fame, and on the other hand, his incapacity to have normal sexual relations, through the creation of a fictional world of horror and destruction in which he found refuge. Poe's fascination with logic would thus be merely an attempt to prove himself rational when he felt he was going insane; and his critical theory merely an attempt to justify his peculiar artistic practice.

The obvious limitations of such a psychoanalytic approach were very sharply and very accurately pointed out by Edmund Wilson in his essay "Poe at Home and Abroad." Krutch, argues Wilson, seriously misunderstands and undervalues Poe's writings, in

> complacently caricaturing them—as the modern school of social psychological biography, of which Mr. Krutch is a typical representative, seems inevitably to tend to caricature the personalities of its subjects. We are nowadays being edified by the spectacle of some of the principal ornaments of the human race exhibited exclusively in terms of their most ridiculous manias, their most disquieting neurosis, and their most humiliating failures. [italics mine]

It is, in other words, the reductionist, stereotypical simplification under which Krutch subsumes the complexities of Poe's art and life that renders this approach inadequate:

> Mr. Krutch quotes with disapproval the statement of President Hadley of Yale, in explaining the refusal of the Hall of Fame to accept Poe among its immortals: "Poe wrote like a drunkard and a man who is not accustomed to pay his debts"; and yet Mr. Krutch himself . . . is almost as unperceptive when he tells us, in effect, that Poe wrote like a dispossessed Southern gentleman and a man with a fixation on his mother.

Subscribing to Wilson's criticism, I would like to indicate briefly some further limitations in this type of psychoanalytic approach to literature. Krutch himself, in fact, points out some of the limits of his method, in his conclusion:

> We have, then, traced Poe's art to an abnormal condition of the nerves and his critical ideas to a rationalized defense of the limitations of his own taste. . . . The question whether or not the case of Poe represents an exaggerated example of the process by which all creation is performed is at best an open question. The extent to which all imaginative works are the result of the unfulfilled desires which spring from either idiosyncratic or universally human maladjustments to life is only beginning to be investigated, and with it is linked the related question of the extent to which all

critical principles are at bottom the systematized and rationalized expression of instinctive tastes which are conditioned by causes often unknown to those whom they affect. The problem of finding an answer to these questions . . . is the one distinctly new problem which the critic of today is called upon to consider. He must, in a word, endeavor to find *the relationship which exists between psychology and aesthetics.* [italics mine]

This, indeed, is the real question, the real challenge which Poe *as poet* (and not as psychotic) presents to the psychoanalytic critic. But this is precisely the very question which is bracketed, never dealt with, in Krutch's study. Krutch discards the question by saying that "the present state of knowledge is not such as to enable" us to give any answers. This remark, however, presupposes—I think mistakenly—that the realm of "aesthetics," of literature and art, might not itself contain some "knowledge" about, precisely, "the relationship between psychology and aesthetics"; it presupposes knowledge as a *given*, external to the literary object and imported into it, and not as a result of a reading-process, that is, of the critic's work upon and with the literary text. It presupposes, furthermore, that a critic's task is not to question but to answer, and that a question that cannot be answered, can also therefore not be asked; that to raise a question, to articulate its thinking power, is not itself a fruitful step which takes some work, some doing, into which the critic could perhaps be guided by the text.

Thus, in claiming that he has traced "Poe's art to an abnormal condition of the nerves," and that Poe's "criticism falls short of psychological truth," Krutch believes that his own work is opposed to Poe's as health is opposed to sickness, as "normality" is opposed to "abnormality," as truth is opposed to delusion. But this ideologically determined, clear-cut opposition between health and sickness is precisely one that Freud's discovery fundamentally unsettles, deconstructs. In tracing Poe's "critical ideas to a rationalized defense of the limitations of his own taste," Krutch is unsuspicious of the fact that his *own* critical ideas about Poe could equally be traced to "a rationalized defense of the limitations of his own taste"; that his doctrine, were it to be true, could equally apply to his own critical enterprise; that if psychoanalysis indeed puts rationality as such in question, it also by the same token puts *itself* in question.

Krutch, in other words, reduces not just Poe but analysis itself into an ideologically biased and psychologically opinionated caricature, missing totally (as is most often the case with "Freudian" critics) the *radicality* of Freud's psychoanalytic insights: their self-critical potential, their power to return upon themselves and to unseat the critic from any condescending, guaranteed, authoritative stance of truth. Krutch's approach does not, then, make sophisticated use of psychoanalytic insights, nor does it address the crucial question of "the relationship between psychology and aesthetics," nor does it see that the crux of this question is not so much in the interrogation of whether or not all artists are necessarily pathological, but of what it is that makes of *art*—not of the artist—an object of *desire* for the public; of what it is that makes for art's *effect*, for the compelling power of Poe's poetry over its readers. The question of what makes poetry lies, indeed, not so much in what it was that made Poe write, but in what it is that *makes us read him* and that ceaselessly drives so many people to *write about him*.

Marie Bonaparte: The approach of clinical diagnosis

In contrast to Krutch's claim that Poe's works, as a literal transcription of his sickness, are only meaningful as the expression of morbidity, bearing "no conceivable relation . . . to the life of any people," Marie Bonaparte, although in turn treating Poe's works as nothing other than the recreations of his neruoses, tries to address the question of Poe's power over his readers through her didactic explanation of the relevancy, on the contrary, of Poe's pathology to "normal" people: the pathological tendencies to which Poe's text gives expression are an exaggerated version of drives and instincts universally human, but which "normal" people have simply repesseed more successfully in their childhood. What fascinates readers in Poe's texts is precisely the unthinkable and unacknowledged but strongly felt *community* of these human—all too human—sexual drives.

 If Marie Bonaparte, unlike Krutch, thus treats Poe with human sympathy, suspending the traditional puritan condemnation and refraining, at least explicitly, from passing judgment on his "sickness," she nonetheless, like Krutch, sets out primarily to diagnose that "sickness" and trace the poetry to it. Like Krutch, she comes up with a clinical "portrait of the artist" which, in claiming to account for the poetry, once again verges on caricature and cannot help but make us smile.

> If Poe was fundamentally necrophilist, as we saw, Baudelaire is revealed as a declared sadist; the former preferred dead prey or prey mortally wounded . . . ; the latter preferred live prey and killing. . . .
>
> How was it then, that despite these different sex lives, Baudelaire the sadist recognised a brother in the necrophilist Poe? . . .
>
> This particular problem raises that of the general relation of sadism to necrophilia and cannot be resolved except by an excursus into the theory of instincts.

Can poetry thus be clinically diagnosed? In setting out to expose didactically the methods of psychoanalytic interpretation, Bonaparte's pioneering book at the same time exemplifies the very naïveté of competence, the distinctive *professional* crudity of what has come to be the classical psychoanalytic treatment of literary texts. Eager to point out the *resemblances* between psychoanalysis and literature, Bonaparte, like most psychoanalytic critics, is totally unaware of the *differences* between the two: unaware of the fact that the differences are as important and as significant for understanding the meeting-ground as are the resemblances, and that those differences also have to be accounted for if poetry is to be understood in its own right. Setting out to study literary texts through the application of psychoanalytic methods, Bonaparte, paradoxically enough but in a manner symptomatic of the whole tradition of applied psychoanalysis, thus remains entirely blind to the very specificity of the object of her research.

It is not surprising that this blind nondifferentiation or confusion of the poetic and the psychotic has unsettled sensitive readers, and that various critics have, in various ways, protested against this all too crude equation of poetry with sickness. The protestations, however, most often fall into the same ideological trap as the psychoanalytical studies they oppose: accepting (taking for granted) the polarity of sickness versus health, of normality versus abnormality, they simply trace Poe's art (in opposition, so they think, to the psychoanalytic claim) to normality as opposed to abnormality, to sanity as opposed to insanity, to the history of ideas rather than that of sexual drives, to a conscious project as opposed to an unconscious one. Camille Mauclair insists upon the fact that Poe's texts are "constructed objectively by a will absolutely in control of itself," and that genius of that kind is "always sane." For Allen Tate,

> The actual emphases Poe gives the perversions are richer in philosophical implication than his psychoanalytic critics have been prepared to see. . . . Poe's symbols refer to a known tradition of thought, an intelligible order, apart from what he was as a man, and are not merely the index to a compulsive neurosis . . . the symbols . . . point towards a larger philosophical dimension.

For Floyd Stovall, the psychoanalytic studies "are not literary critiques at all, but clinical studies of a supposed psychopathic personality":

> I believe the critic should look within the poem or tale for its meaning, and that he should not, in any case, suspect the betrayal of the author's unconscious self until he has understood all that his conscious self has contributed. To affirm that a work of imagination is only a report of the unconscious is to degrade the creative artist to the level of an amanuensis.
>
> I am convinced that all of Poe's poems were composed with conscious art. [p. 183]
>
> "The Raven," and with certain necessary individual differences

every other poem Poe wrote, was the product of conscious effort by a healthy and alert intelligence.

It is obvious that this conception of the mutual exclusiveness, of the clear-cut opposition between "conscious art" and the unconscious, is itself naïve and oversimplified. Nonetheless, Stovall's critique of applied psychoanalysis is relevant to the extent that the psychoanalytic explanation, in pointing exclusively to the author's unconscious sexual fantasies, indeed does not account for Poe's outstanding "conscious art," for his unusual poetic mastery and his ingenious technical and structural self-control. As do its opponents, so does applied psychoanalysis itself fail precisely to account for the dynamic *interaction* between the *unconscious* and the *conscious* elements of art.

If the thrust of the discourse of applied psychoanalysis is, indeed, in tracing poetry to a clinical reality, to *reduce* the poetic to a "cause" outside itself, the crucial limitation of this process of reduction is, however, that the cause, while it may be *necessary*, is by no means a *sufficient* one. "Modern psychiatry," judiciously writes David Galloway, "may greatly aid the critic of literature, but . . . it cannot thus far explain why other men, suffering from deprivations or fears or obsessions similar to Poe's, failed to demonstrate his particular creative talent. Though no doubt Marie Bonaparte was correct in seeing Poe's own art as a defense against madness, we must be wary of identifying the *necessity* for this defense, in terms of Poe's own life, with the *success* of this defense, which can only be measured in his art."

That the discourse of applied psychoanalysis is limited precisely in that it does not account for Poe's poetic *genius* is in fact the crucial point made by Freud himself in his prefatory note to Marie Bonaparte's study:

Foreword

In this book my friend and pupil, Marie Bonaparte, has shown the light of psychoanalysis on the life and work of a great writer with pathologic trends.

Thanks to her interpretative effort, we now realize how many of the characteristics of Poe's works were conditioned by his personality, and can see how that personality derived from intense emotional fixations and painful infantile experiences. *Investigations such as this do not claim to explain creative genius*, but they do reveal the factors which awake it and the sort of subject matter it is destined to choose. . . .

Sigm. Freud

No doubt, Freud's remarkable superiority over some (most) of his disciples—including Marie Bonaparte—proceeds from his acute *awareness* of the very *limitations* of his method, an awareness that in his followers seems most often not to exist.

I would like here to raise a question which, springing out of this limitation of applied psychoanalysis, has, amazingly enough, never been asked as a serious question: is there a way *around* Freud's perspicacious reservation, warning us that studies like those of Bonaparte "do not claim to explain creative genius"? Is there, in other words, a way—a different way—in which psychoanalysis *can* help us to account for poetic genius? Is there an alternative to applied psychoanalysis?—an alternative that would be capable of touching, in a psychoanalytic manner, upon the very specificity of that which constitutes the poetic?

Before endeavoring to articulate the way in which this question might be answered, I would like to examine still another manner in which Poe's text has been psychoanalytically approached. Jacques Lacan's "Seminar" on Poe's short story, "The Purloined Letter."

Jacques Lacan: The approach of textual problematization

"The Purloined Letter," as is well known, is the story of the double theft of a compromising letter, originally sent to the queen. Surprised by the unexpected entrance of the king, the queen leaves the letter on the table in full view of any visitor, where it is least likely to appear suspicious and therefore to attract the king's attention. Enters the Minister D., who, observing the queen's anxiety, and the play of glances between her and the unsuspicious king, analyzes the situation, figures out, recognizing the addressor's handwriting, what the letter is about, and steals it—by substituting for it another letter which he takes from his pocket—under the very eyes of the challenged queen, who can do nothing to prevent the theft without provoking the king's suspicions, and who is therefore reduced to silence. The queen then asks the prefect of police to search the minister's apartment and person, so as to find the letter and restore it to her. The prefect uses every conceivable secret-police technique to search every conceivable hiding place on the minister's premises, but to no avail: the letter remains undiscovered.

Having exhausted his resources, the prefect consults Auguste Dupin, the famous "analyst," as Poe calls him (i.e., an amateur detective who excels in solving problems by means of deductive logic), to whom he tells the whole story. (It is, in fact, from this narration of the prefect of police to Dupin and in turn reported by the first-person narrator, Dupin's friend, who is also present, that we, the readers, learn the story.)

On a second encounter between the prefect of police and Dupin, the latter, to the great surprise of the prefect and of the narrator, produces the purloined letter out of his drawer and hands it to the prefect in return for a large amount of money. The prefect leaves, and Dupin explains to the narrator how he came into possession of the letter: he had deduced that the minister, knowing that his premises would be thoroughly combed by the police, had concluded that the best principle of concealment would be to leave the letter in the open, in full view: in that way the police, searching for hidden secret drawers, would be outwitted, and the letter would not be discovered precisely because it would be too self-evident. On this assumption, Dupin called on the minister in his apartment and, glancing around, soon located the letter most carelessly hanging from the mantelpiece in a card-rack. A little later, a disturbance in the street provoked by a man in Dupin's employ drew the minister to the window, at which moment Dupin quickly replaced the letter with a facsimile, having slipped the real one into his pocket.

I will not enter here into the complexity of the psychoanalytic issues involved in Lacan's "The Seminar on *The Purloined Letter*," nor will I try to deal exhaustively with the nuanced sophistication of the seminar's rhetoric and theoretical propositions; I will confine myself to a few specific points that bear upon the methodological issue of Lacan's psychoanalytic treatment of the literary material.

What Lacan is concerned with at this point of his research is the psychoanalytic problematics of the "repetition-compulsion," as elaborated in Freud's speculative text, *Beyond the Pleasure Principle*. The thrust of Lacan's endeavor, with respect to Poe, is thus to point out—so as to elucidate the nature of Freudian repetition—the way in which the story's plot, its sequence of events (as, for Freud, the sequence of events in a life-story), is entirely contingent on, overdetermined by, a principle of repetition that governs it and inadvertently structures its dramatic and ironic impact. "There are two scenes," remarks Lacan, "the first of which we shall straightway designate the primal scene, . . . since the second may be considered its repetition in the very sense we are considering today." The "primal scene" takes place in the queen's boudoir: it is the theft of the letter from the queen by the minister; the second scene—its repetition—is the theft of the letter from the minister by Dupin, in the minister's hotel.

What constitutes repetition for Lacan, however, is not the mere thematic resemblance of the double *theft*, but the whole structural situation in which the repeated theft takes place: in each case, the theft is the outcome of an intersubjective relationship between three terms; in the first scene, the three participants are the king, the queen, and the minister; in the second, the three participants are the police, the minister, and Dupin. In much the same way as Dupin takes the place of the minister in the first scene (the place of the letter's robber), the minister in the second scene takes the place of the queen in the first (the dispossessed possessor of the letter); whereas the police, for whom the letter remains invisible, take the place formerly occupied by the king. The two scenes thus mirror each other, in that they dramatize the repeated exchange of "three glances, borne by three subjects, incarnated each time by different characters." What is repeated, in other words, is not a

It is instructive to compare Lacan's study of the psychoanalytical repetition compulsion in Poe's text to Marie Bonaparte's study of Poe's repetition compulsion through his text. Although the two analysts study the same author and focus on the same psychoanalytic concept, their approaches are strikingly different. To the extent that Bonaparte's study of Poe has become a classic, a model of applied psychoanalysis which illustrates and embodies the most common understanding of what a psychoanalytic reading of a literary text might be, I would like, in pointing out the differences in Lacan's approach, to suggest the way in which those differences at once put in question the traditional approach and offer an alternative to it.

What does a repetition compulsion repeat?
Interpretation of difference as opposed to interpretation of identity

For Marie Bonaparte, what is compulsively repeated through the variety of Poe's texts is *the same* unconscious fantasy: Poe's (sadonecrophiliac) desire for his dead mother. For Lacan, what is repeated in the text is not the content of a fantasy but the symbolic displacement of a signifier through the insistence of a signifying chain; repetition is not of *sameness* but of *difference*, not of independent terms or of analogous themes but of a structure of differential interrelationships, in which what *returns* is always *other*. Thus, the triangular structure repeats itself only through the *difference* of the characters who successively come to occupy the three positions; its structural significance is perceived only *through* this difference. Likewise, the significance of the letter is situated in its *displacement*, that is, in its repetitive movements toward a *different* place. And the second scene, being, for Lacan, an allegory of analysis, is important not just in that it *repeats* the first scene, but in the way this repetition (like the transferential repetition of a psychoanalytical experience) *makes a difference*: brings about a solution to the problem. Thus, whereas Marie Bonaparte analyzes repetition as the insistence of identity, for Lacan, any possible insight into the reality of the unconscious is contingent upon a perception of repetition, not as a confirmation of identity, but as the insistence of the indelibility of a difference.

An analysis of the signifier as opposed to an analysis of the signified

In the light of Lacan's reading of Poe's tale as itself an allegory of the psychoanalytic reading, it might be illuminating to define the difference in approach between Lacan and Bonaparte in terms of the story. If the purloined letter can be said to be a sign of the unconscious, for Marie Bonaparte the analyst's task is to uncover the letter's *content*, which she believes—as do the police—to be *hidden* somewhere in the real, in some secret biographical *depth.* For Lacan, on the other hand, the analyst's task is not to read the letter's hidden referential content, but to situate the superficial indication of its textual movement, to analyze the paradoxically invisible symbolic evidence of its displacement, its structural insistence, in a signifying chain. "There is such a thing," writes Poe, "as being too profound. Truth is not always in a well. In fact, as regards the most important knowledge, I do believe she is invariably superficial." Espousing Poe's insight, Lacan makes the principle of symbolic evidence the guideline for an analysis not of the signified but of the signifier—for an analysis of the unconscious (the repressed) not as hidden but on the contrary as *exposed*—in language—through a significant (rhetorical) displacement.

This analysis of the signifier, the model of which can be found in Freud's interpretation of dreams, is nonetheless a radical reversal of the traditional expectations and presuppositions involved in the common psychoanalytical approach to literature, and its invariable search for hidden meanings. Indeed, not only is Lacan's reading of "The Purloined Letter" subversive of the traditional model of psychoanalytical reading; it is, in general, a type of reading that is methodologically unprecedented in the whole history of literary criticism. The history of reading has accustomed us to the assumption—usually unquestioned—that reading is finding meaning, that interpretation—of whatever method—can dwell but on the meaningful. Lacan's analysis of the signifier opens up a radically new assumption, an assumption which is nonetheless nothing but an insightful logical and methodological consequence of Freud's discovery: that what *can* be read (and perhaps what *should* be read) is not just meaning, but the lack of meaning; that significance lies not just in consciousness, but, specifically, in its disruption; that the signifier can be analyzed in its effects without its signified being known; that the lack of meaning—the discontinuity in conscious understanding—can and should be interpreted as such, without necessarily being transformed into meaning. "Let's take a look," writes Lacan:

> We shall find illumination in what at first seems to obscure matters: the fact that the tale leaves us in virtually total ignorance of the sender, no less than of the contents, of the letter.
>
> The signifier is not functional. . . . We might even admit that the letter has an entirely different (if no more urgent) meaning for the Queen than the one understood by the Minister. The sequence of events would not be noticeably affected, not even if it were strictly incomprehensible to an uninformed reader.
>
> But that this is the very effect of the unconscious in the precise sense that we teach that the unconscious means that man is inhabited by the signifier.

Thus, for Lacan, what is analytical par excellence is not (as is the case for Bonaparte) the *readable*, but the *unreadable*, and the *effects* of the unreadable. What calls for analysis is the insistence of the unreadable in the text.

Poe, of course, had said it all in his insightful comment, previously quoted, on the nature of what he too—amazingly enough, before the fact—called "the analytical":

> The mental features discoursed of as the analytical are, in themselves, but little susceptible of analysis. We appreciate them only in their effects.

But, oddly enough, what Poe himself had said so strikingly and so explicitly about "the analytical" had itself remained totally unanalyzed, indeed unnoticed, by psychoanalytic scholars before Lacan, perhaps because it, too, according to its own (analytical) logic, had been "a little too self-evident" to be perceived.

A textual as opposed to a biographical approach

The analysis of the signifier implies a theory of textuality for which Poe's biography, or his so-called sickness, or his hypothetical personal psychoanalysis, become irrelevant. The presupposition—governing enterprises like that of Marie Bonaparte—that poetry can be interpreted only as autobiography is obviously limiting and limited. Lacan's textual analysis for the first time offers a psychoanalytical alternative to the previously unquestioned and thus seemingly exclusive biographical approach.

The analyst/author relation:
A subversion of the master/slave pattern and of the doctor/patient opposition

Let us remember how many readers were unsettled by the humiliating and sometimes condescending psychoanalytic emphasis on Poe's "sickness," as well as by an explanation equating the poetic with the psychotic. There seemed to be no doubt in the minds of psychoanalytic readers that if the reading situation could be assimilated to the psychoanalytic situation, the poet was to be equated with the (sick) patient, with the analysand on the couch. Lacan's analysis, however, radically subverts not just this clinical status of the poet, but along with it the "bedside" security of the interpreter. If Lacan is not concerned with Poe's sickness, he is quite concerned, nonetheless, with the *figure of the poet* in the tale, and with the hypotheses made about his specific competence and incompetence. Let us not forget that both the minister and Dupin are said to be poets, and that it is their *poetic* reasoning that the prefect fails to understand and which thus enables both to outsmart

the police. "D———, I presume, is not altogether a fool," comments Dupin
early in the story, to which the prefect of police replies:

> "Not altogether a fool, . . . but then he's a poet, which I take to be only one
> remove from a fool."
> "True," said Dupin, after a long and thoughtful whiff from his
> meerchaum, "although I have been guilty of certain doggerel myself."

A question Lacan does not address could here be raised by emphasizing still
another point that would normally tend to pass unnoticed, since, once again,
it is at once so explicit and so ostentatiously insignificant: why does Dupin say
that he too is *guilty* of poetry? In what way does the status of the poet involve
guilt? In what sense can we understand *the guilt of poetry?*

Dupin, then, draws our attention to the fact that both he and the
minister are poets, a qualification with respect to which the prefect feels that
he can but be condescending. Later, when Dupin explains to the narrator the
prefect's defeat as opposed to his own success in finding the letter, he again
insists upon the prefect's blindness to a logic or to a "principle of concealment" which has to do with poets and thus (it might be assumed) is specifically *poetic*:

> This functionary [the prefect] has been thoroughly mystified; and the
> remote source of his defeat lies in the supposition that the Minister is a *fool*,
> because he has acquired renown as a *poet*. All fools are poets; this the Prefect
> *feels*; and he is merely guilty of a *non distributio medii* in thence inferring that
> all poets are fools.

In Baudelaire's translation of Poe's tale into French, the word *fool* is rendered,
in its strong, archaic sense, as: *fou*, "mad." Here, then, is Lacan's paraphrase
of this passage in the story:

> After which, a moment of derision [on Dupin's part] at the Prefect's error in
> deducing that because the Minister is a poet, he is not far from being mad,
> an error, it is argued, which would consist, . . . simply in a false distribution
> of the middle term, since it is far from following from the fact that all
> madmen are poets.
> Yes indeed. But we ourselves are left in the dark as to the poet's
> superiority in the art of concealment.

Both this passage in the story and this comment by Lacan seem to be
marginal, incidental. Yet the hypothetical *relationship between poetry and
madness* is significantly relevant to the case of Poe and to the other psychoanalytical approaches we have been considering. Could it not be said that the
error of Marie Bonaparte (who, like the prefect, engages in a search for *hidden*
meaning) lies precisely in the fact that, like the prefect once again, she
simplistically *equates* the poetic with the psychotic, and so, blinded by what

she takes to be the poetic *incompetence*, fails to see or understand the specificity of poetic *competence*? Many psychoanalytic investigations diagnosing the poet's sickness and looking for his poetic secret on (or in) his person (as do the prefect's men) are indeed very like police investigations; and like the police in Poe's story, they fail to find the letter, fail to see the textuality of the text.

Lacan, of course, does not say all this—this is not what is at stake in his analysis. All he does is open up still another question where we have believed we have come in possession of some sort of answer:

> Yes indeed. But we ourselves are left in the dark as to the poet's superiority in the art of concealment.

This seemingly lateral question, asked in passing and left unanswered, suggests, however, the possibility of a whole different focus or perspective of interpretation in the story. If "The Purloined Letter" is specifically the story of "the poet's superiority in the art of concealment," then it is not just an allegory of psychoanalysis but also, at the same time, an allegory of poetic writing. And Lacan is himself a poet to the extent that a thought about poetry is what is superiorly concealed in his "Seminar."

In Lacan's interpretation, however, "the poet's superiority" can only be understood as the structural superiority of the third position with respect to the letter: the minister in the first scene, Dupin in the second, both, indeed, poets. But the third position is also—this is the main point of Lacan's analysis—the position of the analyst. It follows that, in Lacan's approach, the status of the poet is no longer that of the (sick) patient but, if anything, that of the analyst. If the poet is still the object of the accusation of being a "fool," his folly—if in fact it does exist (which remains an open question)— would at the same time be the folly of the analyst. The clear-cut opposition between madness and health, or between doctor and patient, is unsettled by the odd functioning of the purloined letter of the unconscious, which no one can possess or master. "There is no metalanguage," says Lacan: there is no language in which interpretation can itself escape the effects of the unconscious; the interpreter is not more immune than the poet to unconscious delusions and errors.

Implication, as opposed to application, of psychoanalytic theory

Lacan's approach no longer falls into the category of what has been called "applied psychoanalysis," since the concept of "application" implies a relation of *exteriority* between the applied science and the field which it is supposed, unilaterally, to inform. Since, in Lacan's analysis, Poe's text serves to *re-interpret Freud* just as Freud's text serves to interpret Poe; since psychoanalytic theory and the literary text mutually inform—and displace—each other; since the very position of the interpreter—of the analyst—turns out to be not *outside*, but *inside* the text, there is no longer a clear-cut opposition or a well-defined border between literature and psychoanalysis: psychoanalysis could be intraliterary just as much as literature is intrapsychoanalytic. The methodological stake is no longer that of the *application* of psychoanalysis *to* literature, but rather, of their *interimplication in* each other.

If I have dealt at length with Lacan's innovative contribution and with the different methodological example of his approach, it is not so much to set this example up as a new model for imitation, but rather to indicate the way in which it suggestively invites us to go beyond itself (as it takes Freud beyond itself), the way in which it opens up a whole new range of as yet untried possibilities for the enterprise of reading. Lacan's importance in my eyes does not, in other words, lie specifically in the new dogma his "school" proposes, but in his outstanding demonstration that *there is more than one way* to implicate psychoanalysis in literature; that *how to* implicate psychoanalysis in literature is itself a question for interpretation, a challenge to the ingenuity and insight of the interpreter, and not a *given* that can be taken in any way for granted; that what is of analytical relevance in a text is not necessarily and not exclusively "the unconscious of the poet," let alone his sickness or his problems in life; that to situate in a text the analytical as such—to situate the object of analysis or the textual point of its implication—is not necessarily to recognize a *known*, to find an answer, but also, and perhaps more challengingly, to locate an *unknown*, to find a question.

THE POE-ETIC ANALYTICAL

Let us now return to the crucial question we left in suspension earlier, after having raised it by reversing Freud's reservation concerning Marie Bonaparte's type of research: *can* psychoanalysis give us an insight into the specificity of the poetic? We can now supplement this question with a second one: where can we situate the analytical with respect to Poe's poetry?

The answers to these questions, I would suggest, might be sought in two directions. (1) In a direct reading of a poetic text by Poe, trying to locate in the poem itself a signifier of poeticity and to analyze its functioning and its effects; to analyze—in other words—how poetry as such works through signifiers (to the extent that signifiers, as opposed to meanings, are always signifiers of the unconscious). (2) In an analytically informed reading of literary history itself, inasmuch as its treatment of Poe obviously constitutes a (literary) *case history*. Such a reading has never, to my knowledge, been undertaken with respect to any writer: never has literary history itself been viewed as an analytical object, as a subject for a psychoanalytic interpretation. And yet it is overwhelmingly obvious, in a case like Poe's, that the discourse of literary history itself points to some unconscious determinations which structure it but of which it is not aware. What is the unconscious of literary history? Can the question of *the guilt of poetry* be relevant to that unconscious? Could literary history be in any way considered a repetitive unconscious *transference* of the guilt of poetry?

Literary history, or more precisely, the critical discourse surrounding Poe, is indeed one of the most visible ("self-evident") *effects* of Poe's poetic signifier, of his text. Now, how can the question of the peculiar effect of Poe be dealt with analytically? My suggestion is: by locating what seems to be unreadable or incomprehensible in this effect; by situating the most prominent discrepancies or discontinuities in the overall critical discourse concerning Poe, the most puzzling critical contradictions, and by trying to interpret those contradictions as symptomatic of the unsettling specificity of the Poe-etic effect, as well as of the necessary contingence of such an effect on the unconscious.

Before setting out to explore and to illustrate these two directions for research, I would like to recapitulate the primary historical contradictions analyzed at the opening of this study as a first indication of the nature of the poetic. According to its readers' contradictory testimonies, Poe's poetry, let it be recalled, seemed to be at once the most *irresistible* and the most *resisted* poetry in literary history. Poe is felt to be at once the most unequaled master of "conscious art" *and* the most tortuous unconscious case, as such doomed to remain "the perennial victim of the *idée fixe*, and of amateur psychoanalysis." Poetry, I would thus argue, is precisely the effect of a deadly struggle between consciousness and the unconscious; it has to do with resistance and with what can neither be resisted nor escaped. Poe is a symptom of poetry to the extent that poetry is both what most resists a psychoanalytical interpretation and what most depends on psychoanalytical effects.

Chronology

1809   Born in Boston, January 19, as the second of three children of David Poe and his wife, Elizabeth Arnold, both actors. Poe's father abandoned the family, all too soon.

1811   Death of Poe's mother in Richmond, Virginia. The children are taken into diverse households, Edgar into that of John Allan, a Richmond merchant. Not legally adopted, he is nevertheless renamed Edgar Allan.

1815–20   Resident, with the Allans, first in Scotland, then in London.

1820–25   Educated in private schools, after return of Allans to Virginia.

1826   Enters University of Virginia (founded by Jefferson the year before) where he studies languages. Gambling debts compel him to leave, after Allan refuses to pay them.

1827   Enlists in army in Boston, where his first book, *Tamerlane and Other Poems*, appears and is ignored.

1828–29   Honorably discharged as sergeant major and lives in Baltimore, where *Al Aaraaf, Tamerlane and Minor Poems* is published.

1830–31   Enters West Point in May, 1830; does well in studies, but is expelled in January, 1831. Lives in Baltimore with his father's sister, Maria Clemm, and her daughter Virginia, then eight years old. Begins to write tales.

1832–35   Tutors cousin Virginia Clemm, while continuing to write stories. Death of John Allan, with neglect of Poe in his will. Poe writes book reviews for *Southern Literary Messenger*, and becomes editorial assistant on magazine. Moves to Richmond with Virginia and Mrs. Clemm, and becomes editor of the journal.

1836   May marriage to Virginia Clemm, who was not yet fourteen; her mother stayed on as housekeeper. Busy with writing or revising reviews, poems and stories for the *Messenger*.

1837–38   Resigns from *Messenger* and moves himself and household to New York City, where he is unable to secure editorial work. Publishes "Ligeia" and in July, 1838, *Pym*. Moves household to Philadelphia.

1839–40   Works for *Gentleman's Magazine*, where he prints "William Wilson" and "The Fall of the House of Usher." Publishes the two volume *Tales of the Grotesque and Arabesque* in Philadelphia, late in 1839. Fired by his employer and fails to found his own magazine.

1841–42   Is employed as an editor of *Graham's Magazine*, where he prints "The Murders in the Rue Morgue." In January, 1842, Virginia Poe suffers a burst blood vessel while singing. She survives, but is never the same.

1843–45   Rise in Poe's popularity with the prize-winning "The Gold Bug." Moves to New York City and helps edit the *Evening Mirror*, where "The Raven" is printed in January, 1845, and causes a sensation. *Tales* published in July, 1845, *The Raven and Other Poems* that November. Engages in literary quarrel, falsely accusing Longfellow of plagiarism. Virginia's condition worsens. Becomes owner and editor of the *Broadway Journal*.

1846   Abandons *Broadway Journal* because of his depression and financial problems. Moves household to Fordham, New York.

1847   Death of Virginia on January 30. Poe becomes very sick, but is nursed by Mrs. Clemm and recovers.

1848   Proposes marriage to the poet Sarah Helen Whitman, who later breaks off the relationship. Publishes *Eureka* in June.

1849   A year of rapid decline, marked by heavy drinking and paranoid delusions. Travels to Richmond, where he is engaged to Elmira Royster Shelton. Sails to Baltimore, and vanishes. Discovered delirious outside polling booth on October 3, thus suggesting subsequent legend that he was dragged from poll to poll as an alcoholic "repeater." Dies on October 7, ostensibly of "congestion of the brain."

Contributors

HAROLD BLOOM, Sterling Professor of the Humanities at Yale University, is the author of *The Anxiety of Influence, Poetry and Repression* and many other volumes of literary criticism. His forthcoming study, *Freud: Transference and Authority*, attempts a full-scale reading of all of Freud's major writings. He is the general editor of the Chelsea House Library of Literary Criticism.

PAUL VALÉRY is universally regarded as the greatest French poet and man-of-letters of this century. His lifetime (1871–1945) spans the major period of modernist literature, where his only rivals would have to be Rilke, Yeats, Stevens and Montale. Valéry must also be judged to possess the most advanced critical consciousness of his age.

D.H. LAWRENCE was equally powerful as novelist and poet. His principal achievements as a novelist were *The Rainbow* and *Women In Love*. An uneven polemicist and essayist, his *Studies in Classic American Literature* may nevertheless be the single most illuminating book on the American literary imagination.

ALLEN TATE was the representative Southern poet and critic of our time. He is remembered also for his novel, *The Fathers*. His most influential collection of essays remains his aptly titled *The Man of Letters in the Modern World*.

RICHARD WILBUR is one of the principal lyric poets of his generation, and the most accomplished translator of Molière into English.

CLARK GRIFFITH, Professor of English at Iowa, is the author of *The Long Shadow: Emily Dickinson's Tragic Poetry* and of many essays on modern American poetry.

DANIEL HOFFMAN, Professor of English at the University of Pennsylvania, is widely known both as poet and as critic. His major work to date is the long poem, *Brotherly Love*.

JOHN T. IRWIN, chairman of the Writing Seminars at Johns Hopkins University, is the author of a remarkable triangular work, of which *American Hieroglyphics* is the third part, the other two being his study of Faulkner, *Doubling and Incest/Repetition and Revenge*, and the poems published as *The Heisenberg Variations*, under the name of John Bricuth.

SHOSHANA FELMAN is Professor of French at Yale. Her essay on Poe's poetry and psychoanalysis is the Introduction to her forthcoming *Poetry and Psychoanalysis: The Future of Repetition.*

Bibliography

Auden, W.H., ed. "Introduction." In *Selected Prose and Poetry*. New York: Rinehart, 1950.

Bonaparte, Marie. *The Life and Works of Edgar Allan Poe*. Translated by John Rodker. London: Imago Publishing Co., 1949.

Carlson, Eric W., ed. *The Recognition of Edgar Allan Poe*. Ann Arbor: University of Michigan Press, 1966.

Davidson, Edward Hutchins. *Poe: A Critical Study*. Cambridge: Harvard University Press, Belknap Press, 1957.

Eliot, Thomas Stearns. *From Poe to Valéry*. New York: Harcourt-Brace, 1948.

Hoffman, Daniel, *Poe Poe Poe Poe Poe Poe Poe*. Garden City, N.Y.: Doubleday, 1972.

Howarth, William, ed. *Twentieth Century Interpretations of Poe's Tales*. Englewood Cliffs, N.J.: Prentice-Hall, 1971.

Huxley, Aldous. *Music at Night and Other Essays*. London: The Fountain Press, 1931.

Irwin, John T. *American Hieroglyphics*. New Haven: Yale University Press, 1980.

Ketterer, David. *The Rationale of Deception in Poe*. Baton Rouge: Louisiana State University Press, 1979.

Lacan, Jacques. "The Seminar on 'The Purloined Letter.'" Translated by J. Mehlman. *Yale French Studies* 48 (1972).

Levin, Harry. *The Power of Blackness: Hawthorne, Poe, Melville*. New York: Knopf, 1958.

Mabbot, Thomas Ollive, ed. *Collected Works of Edgar Allan Poe*. Cambridge: Harvard University Press, Belknap Press, 1969–78.

Mankowitz, Wolf. *The Extraordinary Mr. Poe*. New York: Summit Books, 1978.

Ostrom, John, ed. *The Letters of Edgar Allan Poe*. Cambridge: Harvard University Press, 1948.

Pollin, Burton R., ed. *The Imaginary Voyages: In the Collected Works of Edgar Allan Poe*. Boston: G.K. Hall, 1981.

Quinn, Arthur Hobson. *Edgar Allan Poe: A Critical Biography*. New York: Appleton-Century-Crofts, 1963.

Quinn, Patrick Francis. *The French Face of Edgar Poe*. Carbondale: Southern Illinois University Press, 1957.

Regan, Robert, ed. *Poe: A Collection of Critical Essays*. Englewood Cliffs, N.J.: Prentice-Hall, 1967.

Stovall, Floyd, ed. *The Poems of Edgar Allan Poe*. Charlottesville: University Press of Virginia, 1965.

Tate, Allen. *The Forlorn Demon*. Chicago: Ayer Co., 1953.

Wagenknecht, Edward Charles. *Edgar Allan Poe: The Man Behind the Legend.* New York: Oxford University Press, 1963.

Whitman, Sarah Helen Power. *Poe's Helen Remembers.* Edited by John Carl Miller. Charlottesville: University Press of Virginia, 1979.

Wilson, Edmund. *The Shores of Light.* New York: Farrar, Strauss and Giroux, 1952.

Woodberry, George Edward. *Edgar Allan Poe.* Boston, New York: Houghton, Mifflin and Co., 1885.

Woodson, Thomas, ed. *Twentieth Century Interpretations of The Fall of the House of Usher.* Englewood Cliffs, N.J.: Prentice-Hall, 1969.

Acknowledgments

"Americanizing the Abyss" by Harold Bloom from *The New York Review of Books* 31, 15 (October 11, 1984), copyright © 1984 by *The New York Review of Books*. Reprinted by permission.

"On Poe's 'Eureka' " by Paul Valéry from *Variety* 1, translated by Malcolm Cowley, copyright © 1927 by Harcourt Brace Jovanovich, Inc. Reprinted by permission.

"The Angelic Imagination" by Allen Tate from *Collected Essays*, copyright © 1952 by *The Kenyon Review* (Summer 1952). Reprinted by permission of Helen H. Tate and *The Kenyon Review*.

"Edgar Allan Poe" by D.H. Lawrence from *Studies in Classic American Literature* by D.H. Lawrence, copyright © 1923 by The Viking Press. Reprinted by permission.

"The House of Poe" by Richard Wilbur from *Anniversary Lectures 1959*, copyright © 1966 by Richard Wilbur. Reprinted by permission.

"Poe's 'Ligeia' and the English Romantics" by Clark Griffith from *University of Toronto Quarterly* 24 (1954), copyright © 1954 by University of Toronto Press. Reprinted by permission of the author and the University of Toronto Press. The notes have been omitted.

"The Marriage Group" by Daniel Hoffman from *Poe Poe Poe Poe Poe Poe Poe* by Daniel Hoffman, copyright © 1972 by Daniel Hoffman. Reprinted by permission of the author.

"The White Shadow" by John T. Irwin from *American Hieroglyphics* by John T. Irwin, copyright © 1980 by Yale University Press. Reprinted by permission.

"On Reading Poetry: Reflections on the Limits and Possibilities of Psychoanalytical Approaches" by Shoshana Felman from *The Literary Freud: Mechanisms of Defense and the Poetic Will* by Shoshana Felman, copyright © 1980 by Shoshana Felman. Reprinted by permission.

Index

Tennyson, Alfred, Lord
    as subject of Poe's criticism, 12
Thompson, John R., 120
Thoreau, Henry David, 2, 105, 110
Timaeus, 117
Timrod, Henry
    comparison with Poe, 2
"To a Skylark," 2
torture, 34
transcendentalism, 72, 74–78
transference, 132
transfiguration, 112
transmigration of souls, 90
truth, 17
Tuckerman, Frederick Goddard
    comparison with Poe, 2
"Tunnel, The," 13
Twain, Mark, 3

U
"Ulalume," 2
unconscious, 62
    relationship to art, 128
    relationship to sleep and death, 109
universe
    aesthetic theories of Poe, 53–54

V
vagina
    symbolism, 85, 86
Valéry, Paul, 15–20
    admiration of Poe, 1, 7, 13, 41, 48
    influenced by Poe, 121, 122
vampirism
    element of Poe's works, 24–26, 29,
    32, 36, 90
ventilation
    symbolism in Poe, 65
Very, Jones, 2

vortex
    symbolism in Poe's works, 53
"Vulgarity in Literature," 121
vulture
    symbolism, 94

W
Walden, 105
Warburton, Bishop, 109
Warren, Robert Penn
    view of Emerson, 5
wealth, 64
*Week on the Concord and Merrimack Rivers,
    A*, 110
"White Shadow, The," 103–18
Whitman, Sarah Helen
    association with Poe, 10
Whitman, Walt, 2, 11
Whittier, John Greenleaf, 2
Wilbur, Richard, 51–69
Wilde, Oscar
    literary criticism, 12
will, 24, 26, 29, 34, 42, 44, 94–96
    Christian philosophy, 114, 115
    philosophy of Poe, 36, 37
"William Wilson," 3, 33, 48, 56
    architectural symbolism, 62
    autobiographical elements, 52
    duality of human nature, 69
Wilson, Edmund, 124
winding
    aspect of Poe's tales, 61
window
    significance in Poe's works, 65
Winters, Yvor, 5, 122
womb
    symbolism, 86
women, 82
Wordsworth, William, 110, 111